Colorblind Perspective

Being colorblind gives an advantage when composing black & white... less confusion.

This special collection exhibits the lonely freedom of a hidden perspective.

All images presented genuine without edits. Color sacrificed through a unique process.

info@ BEACHNOISE.com

I0494714

Jh Fleming

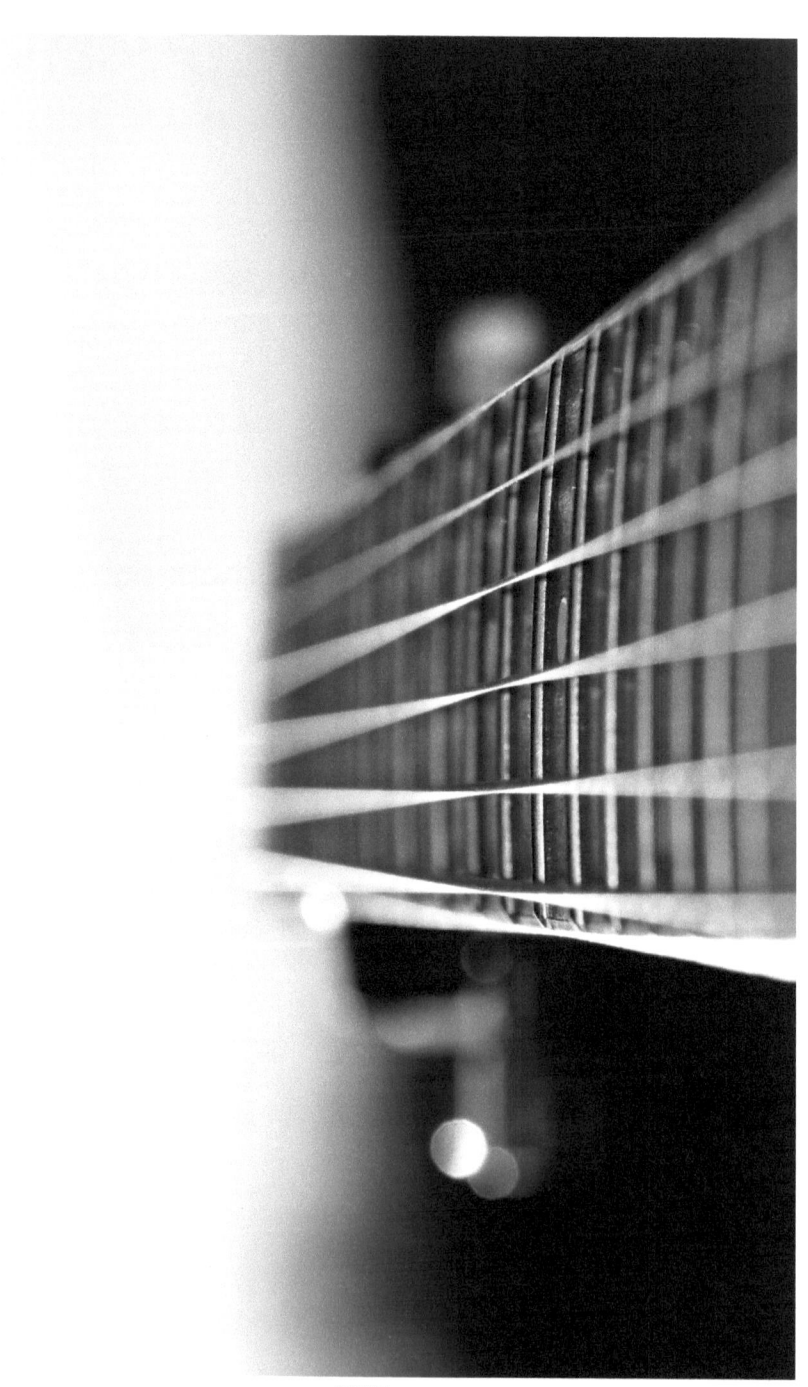

0351

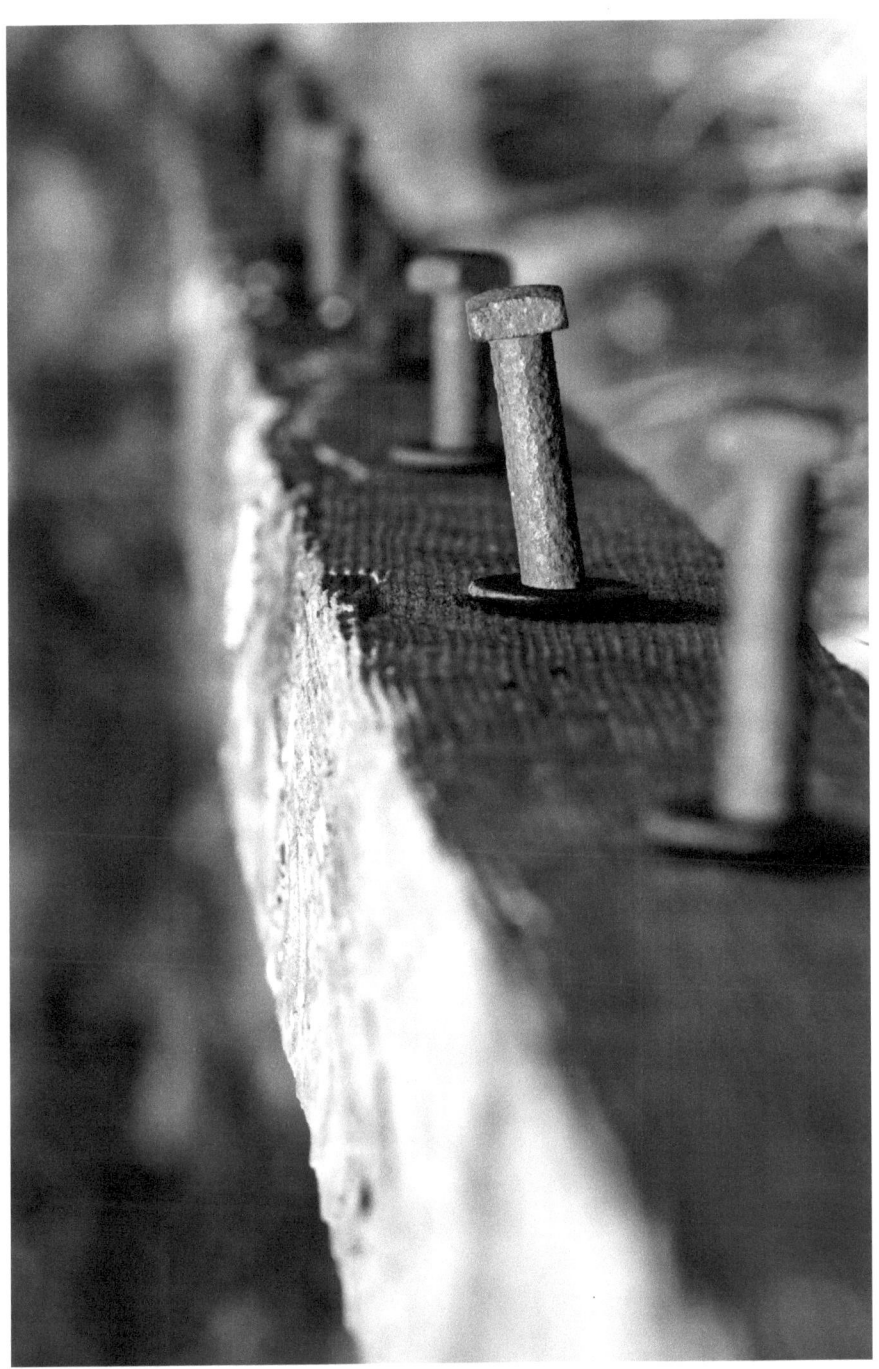

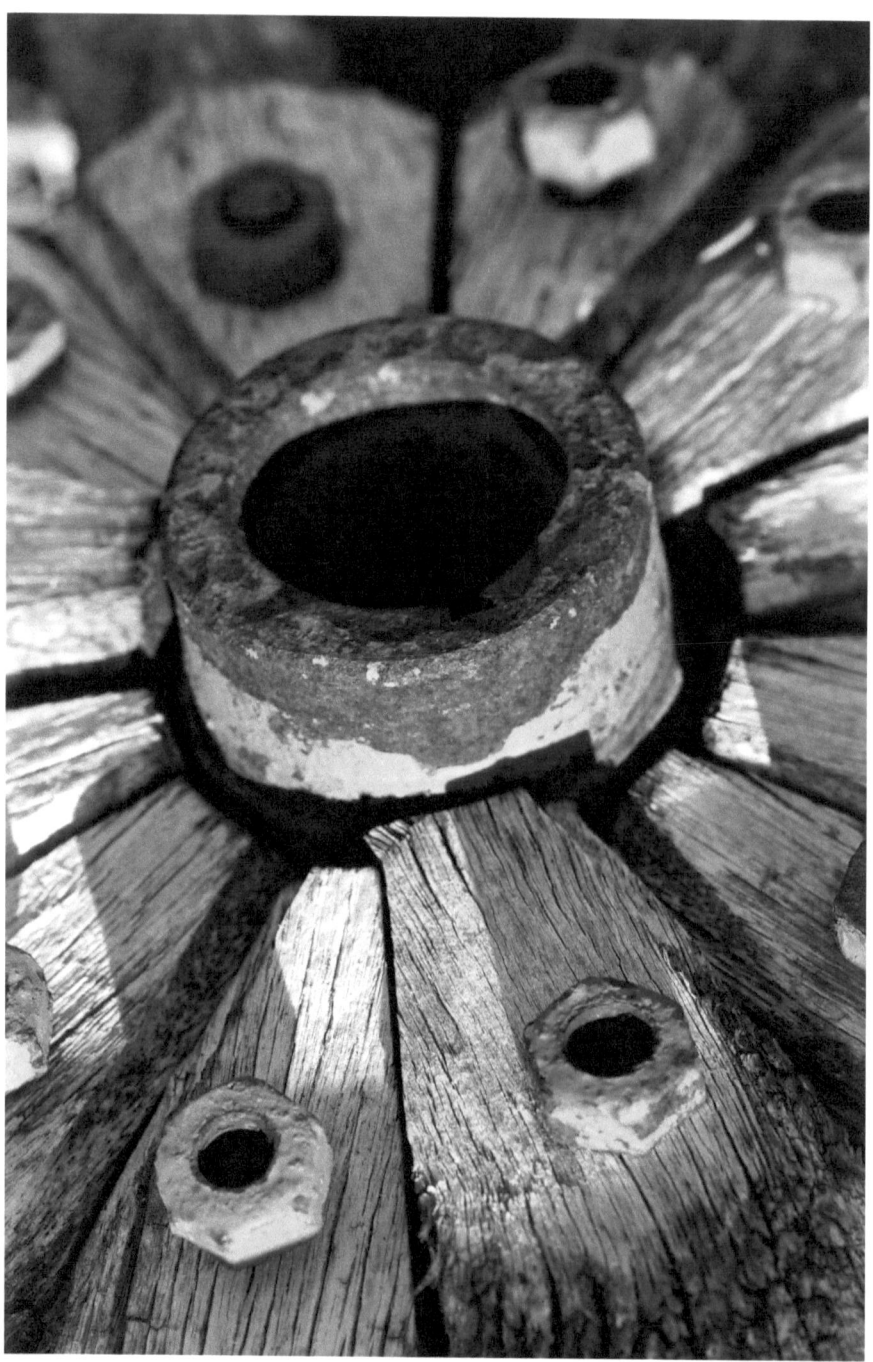

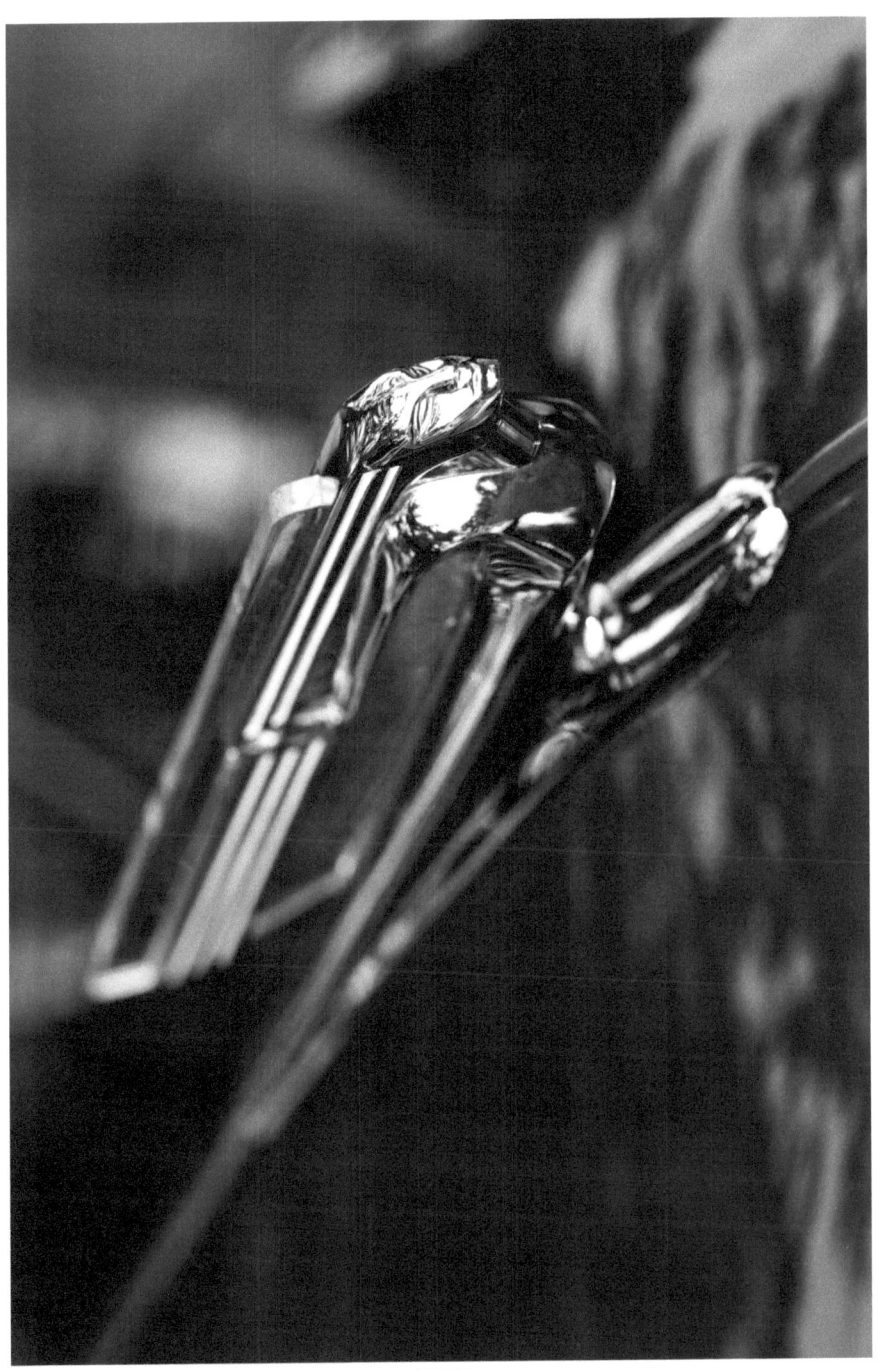

0705

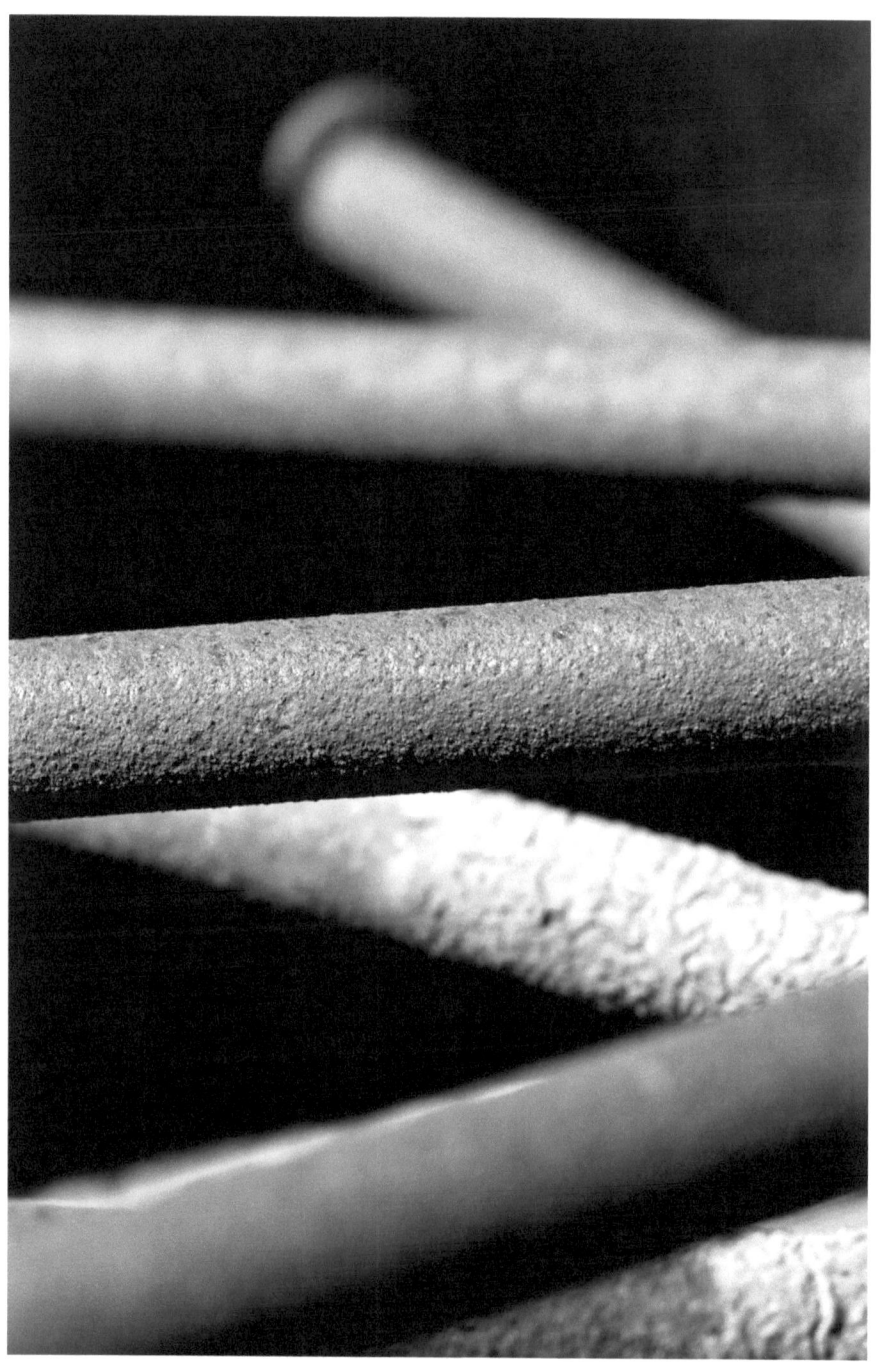

0780

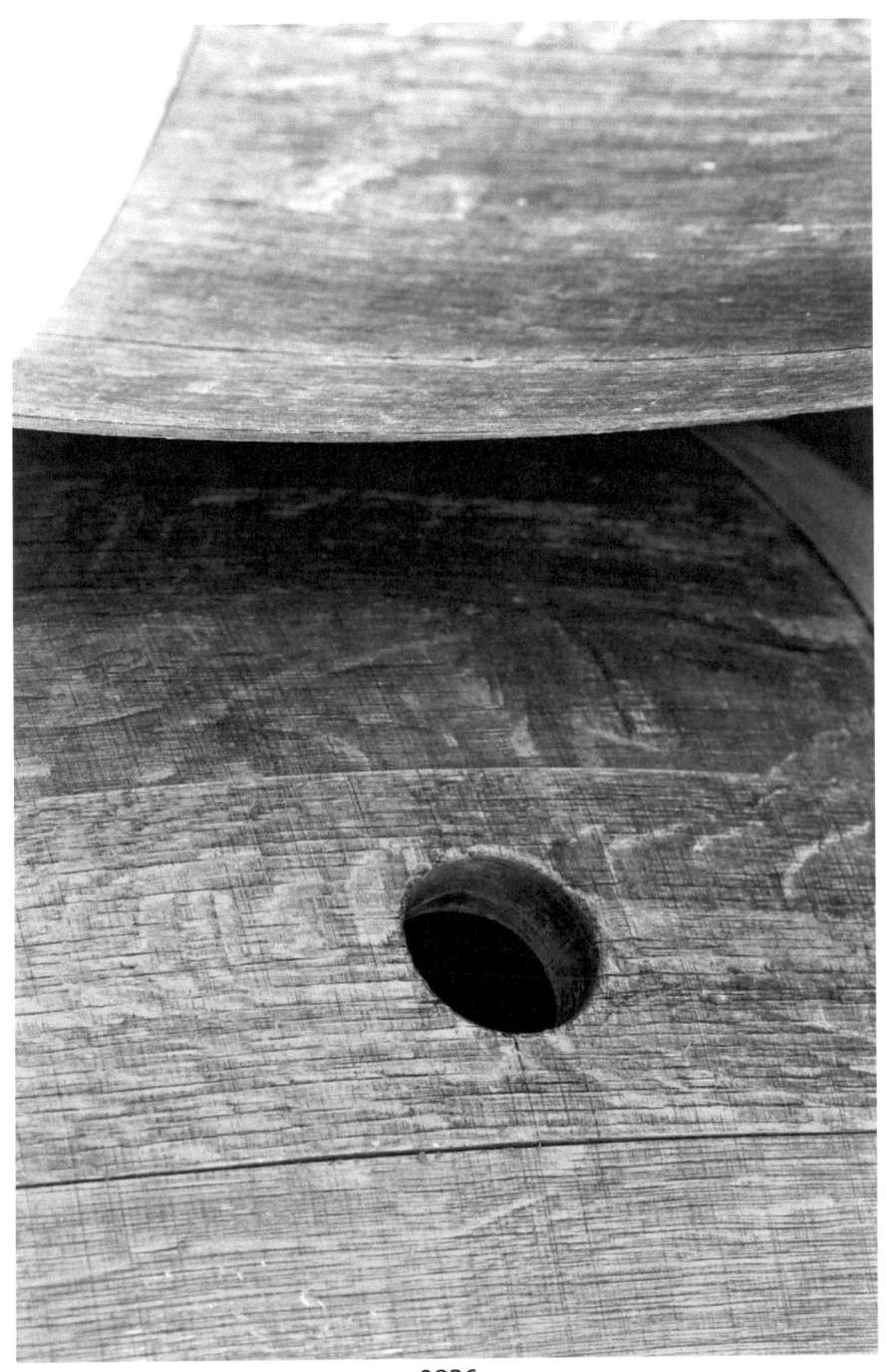

0826

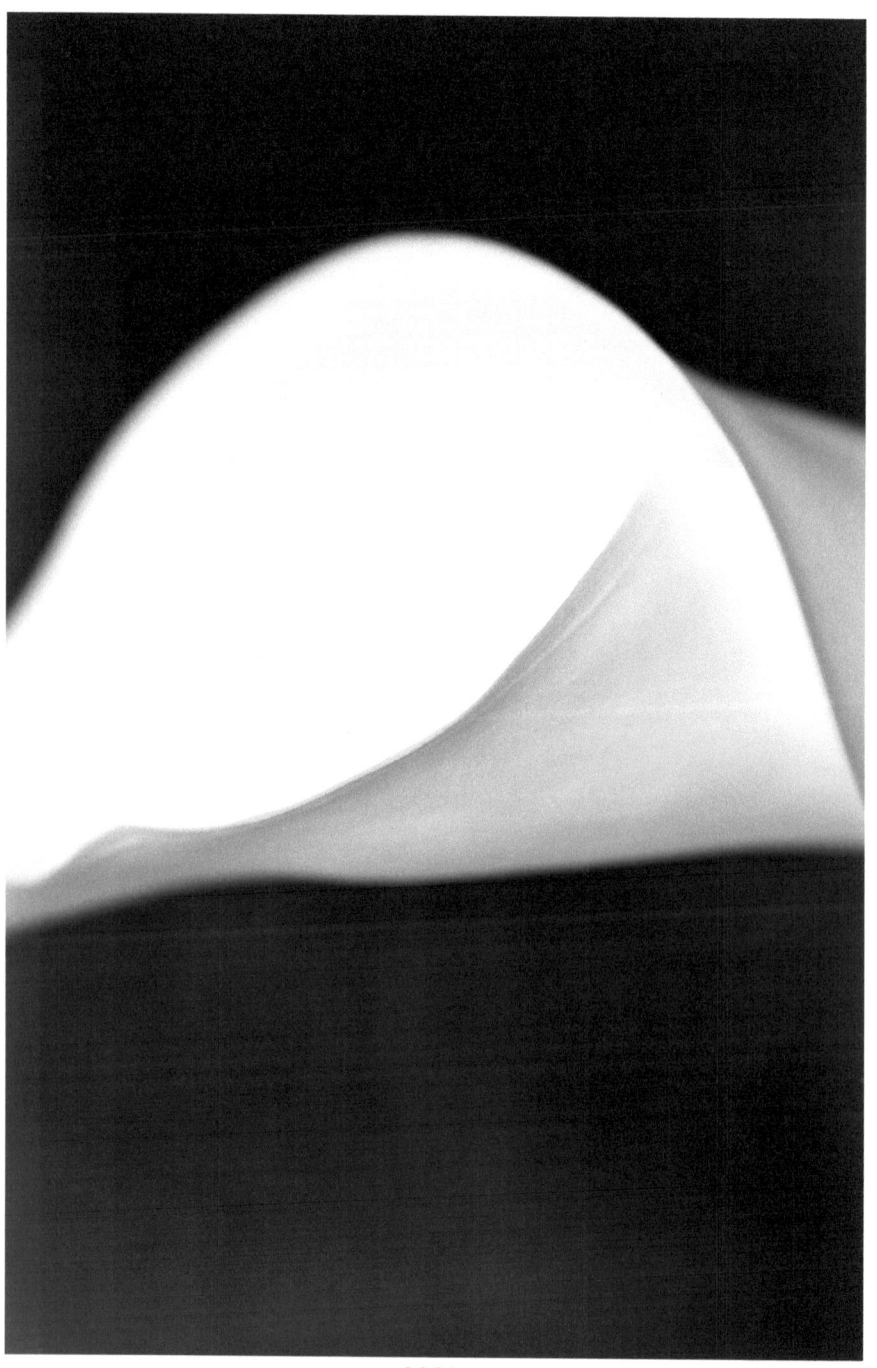

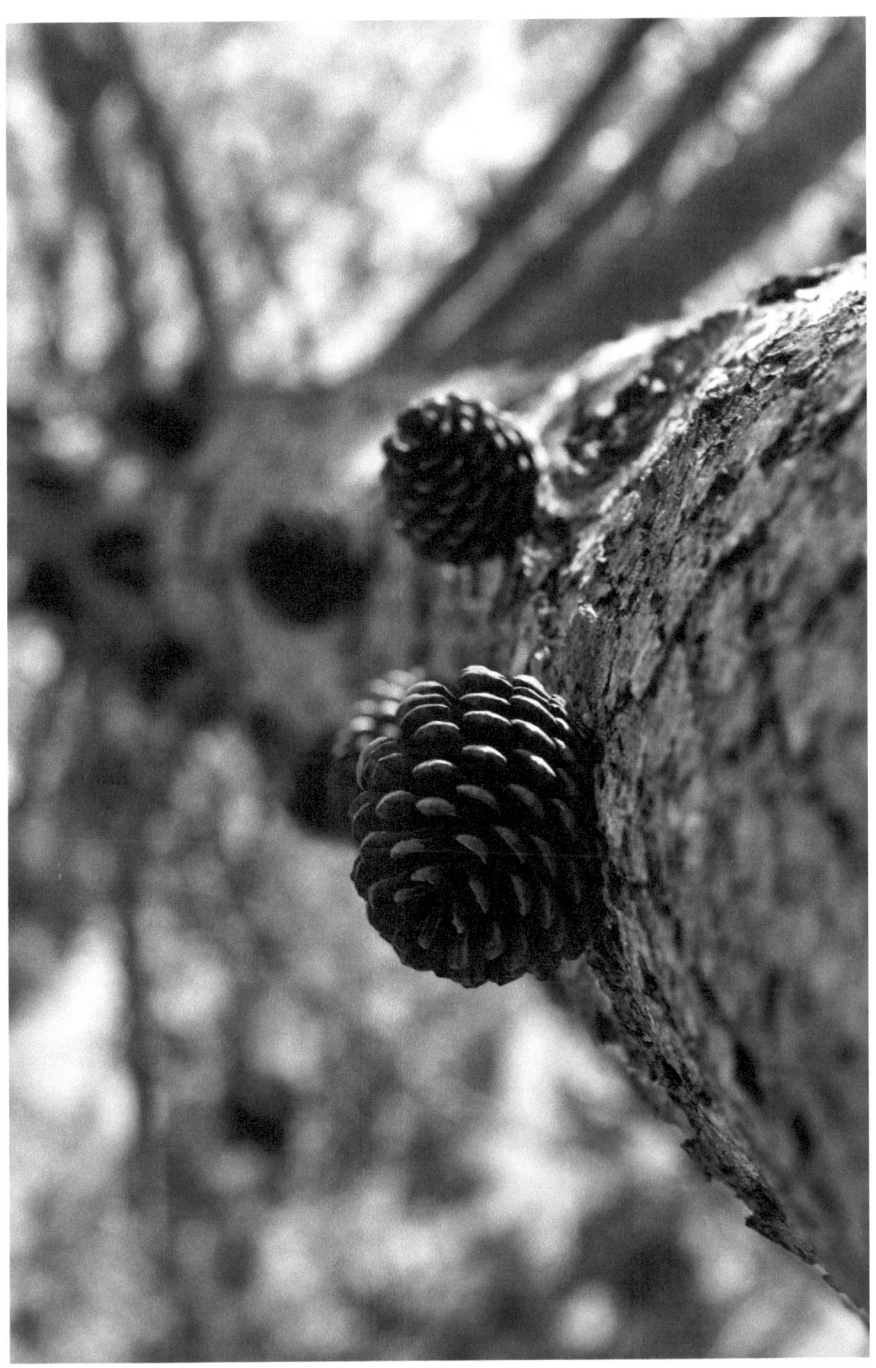

0938

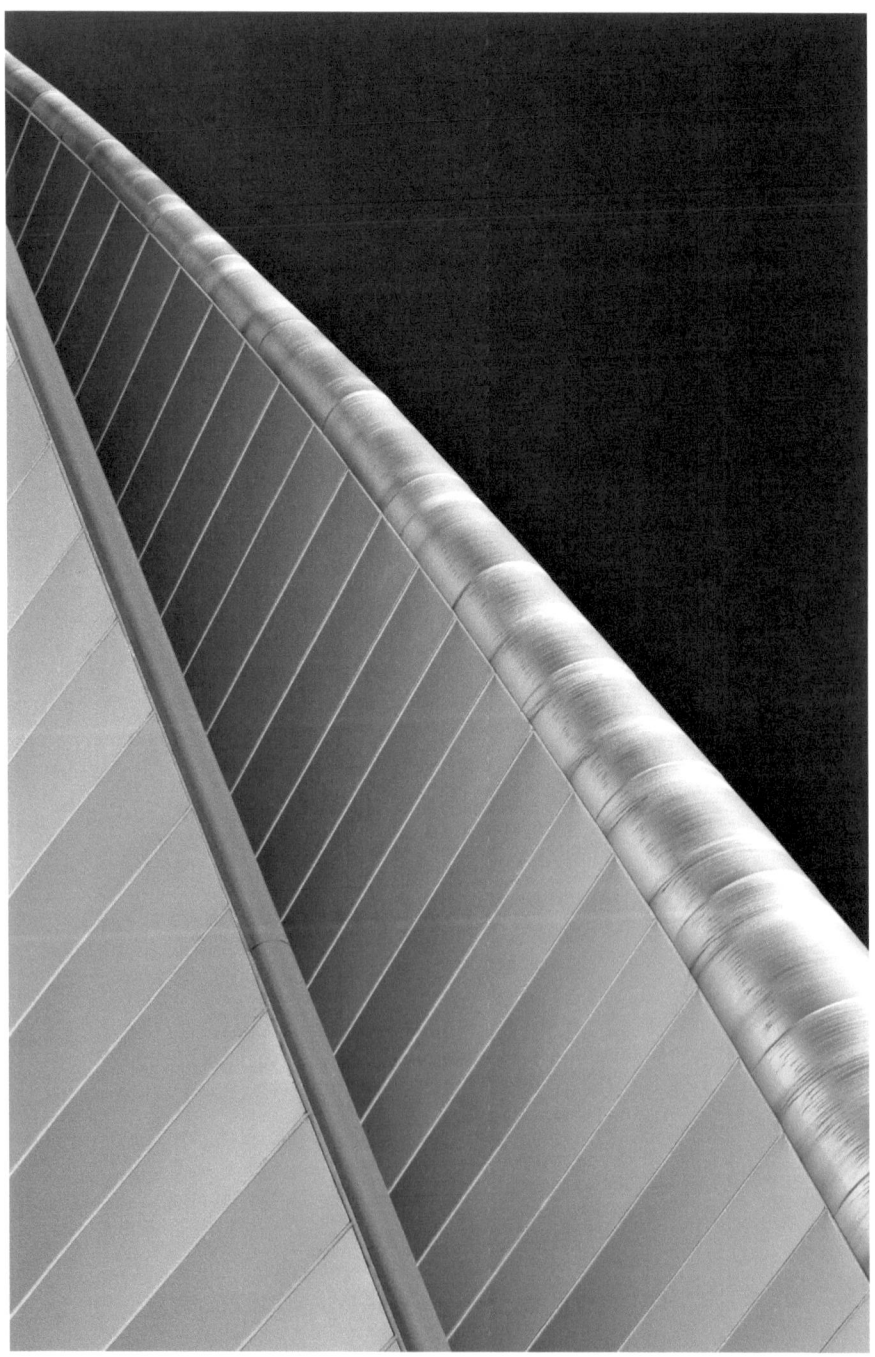

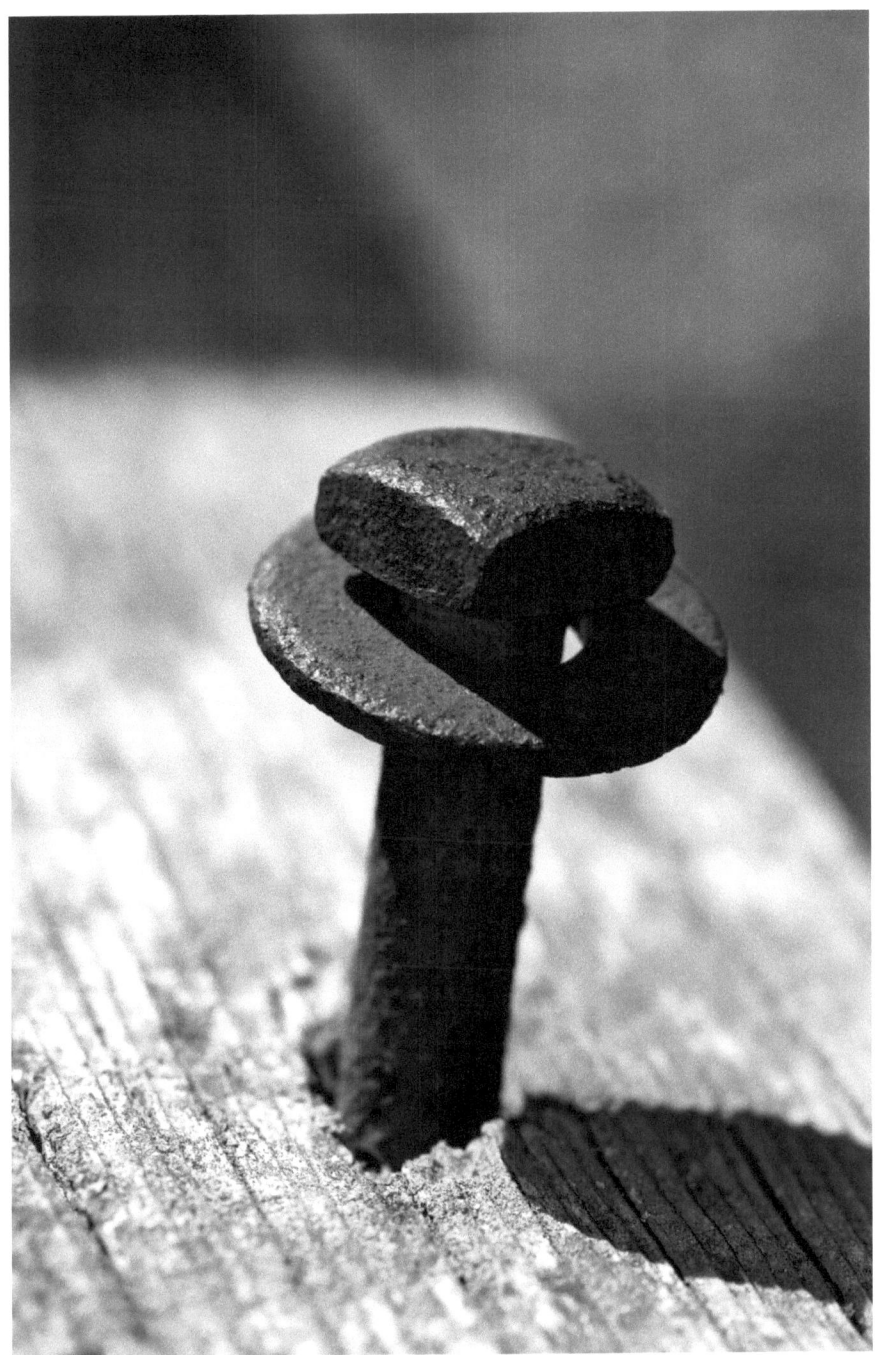

1173

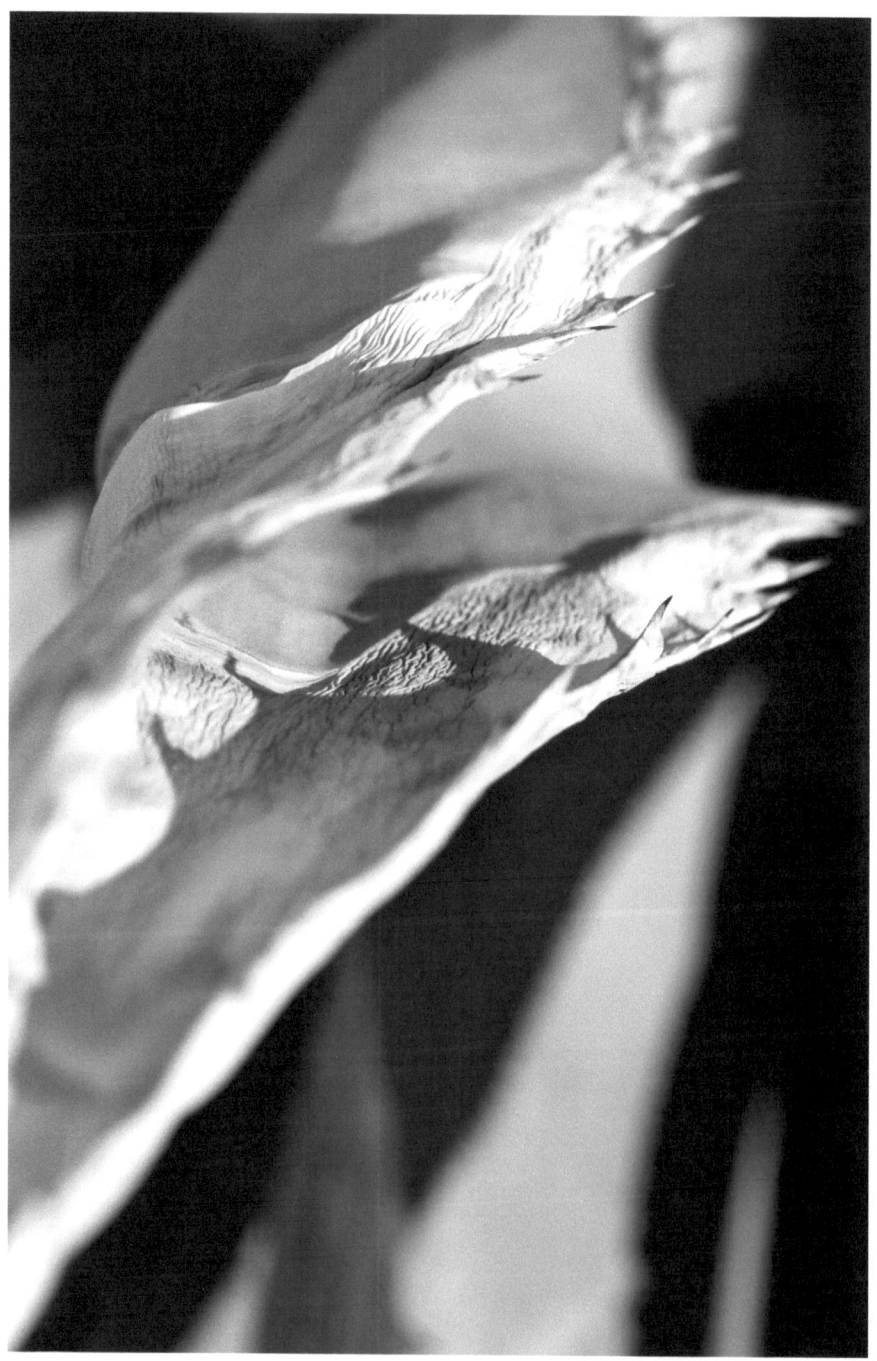

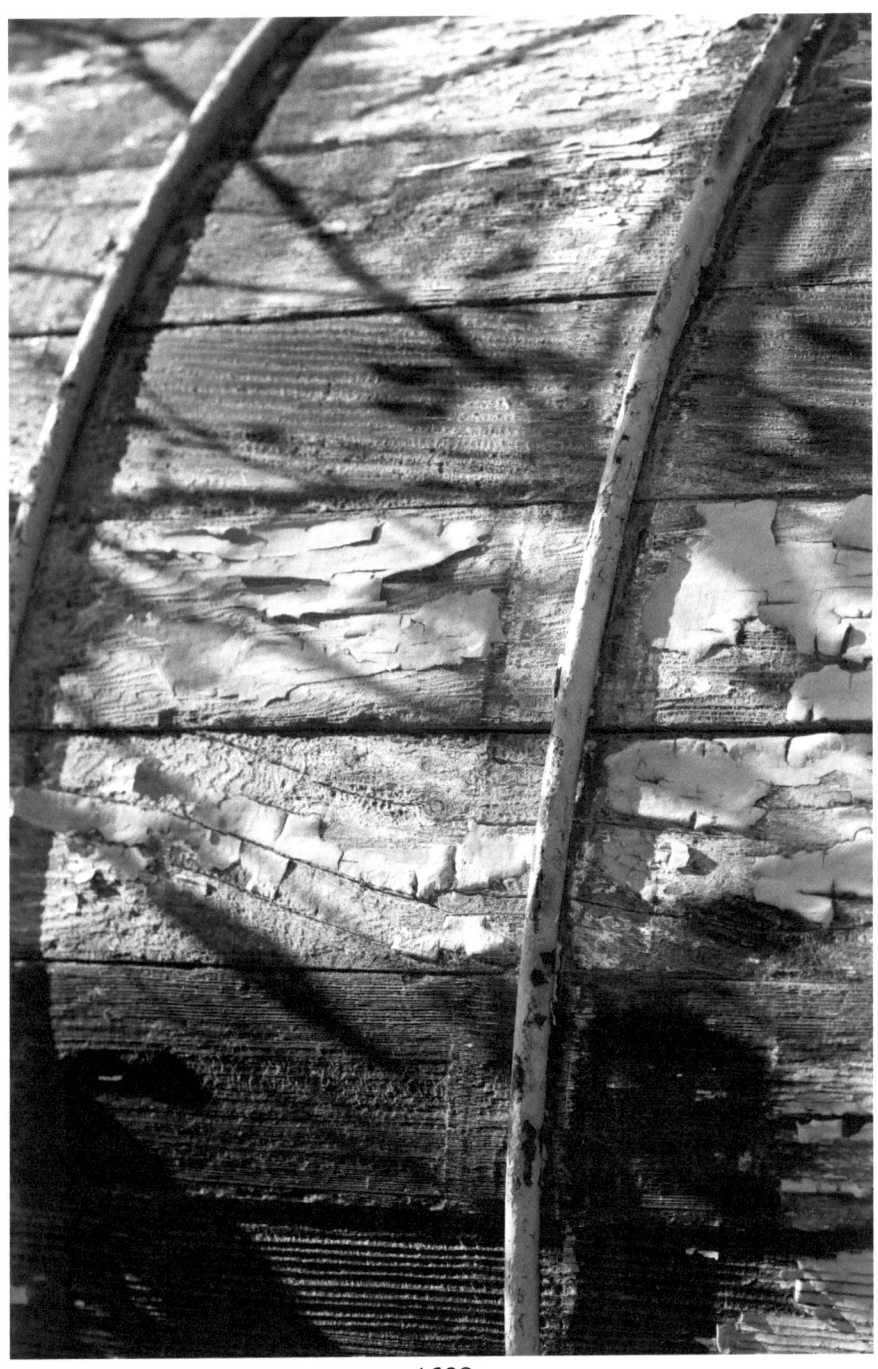

1608

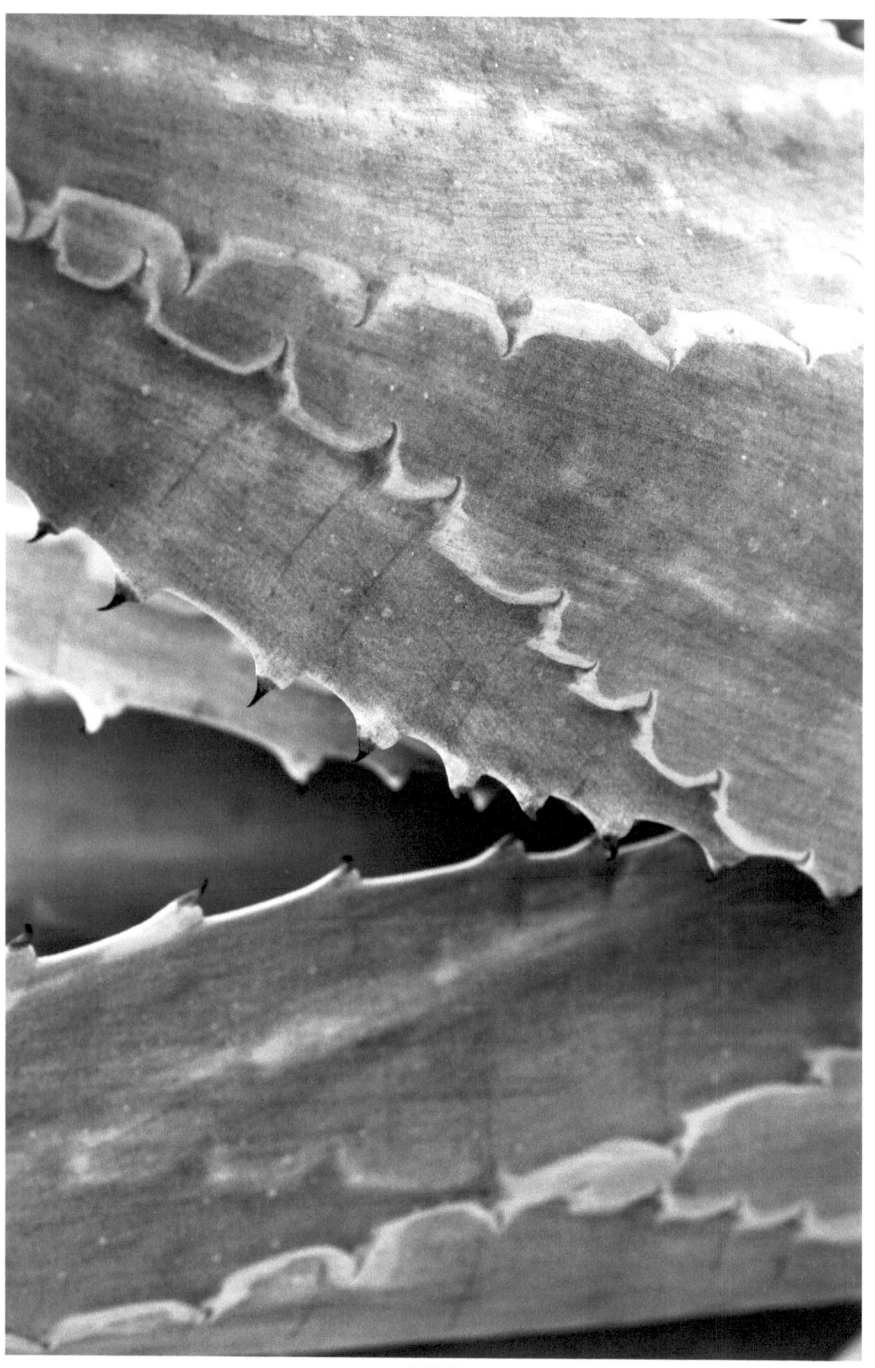

1976

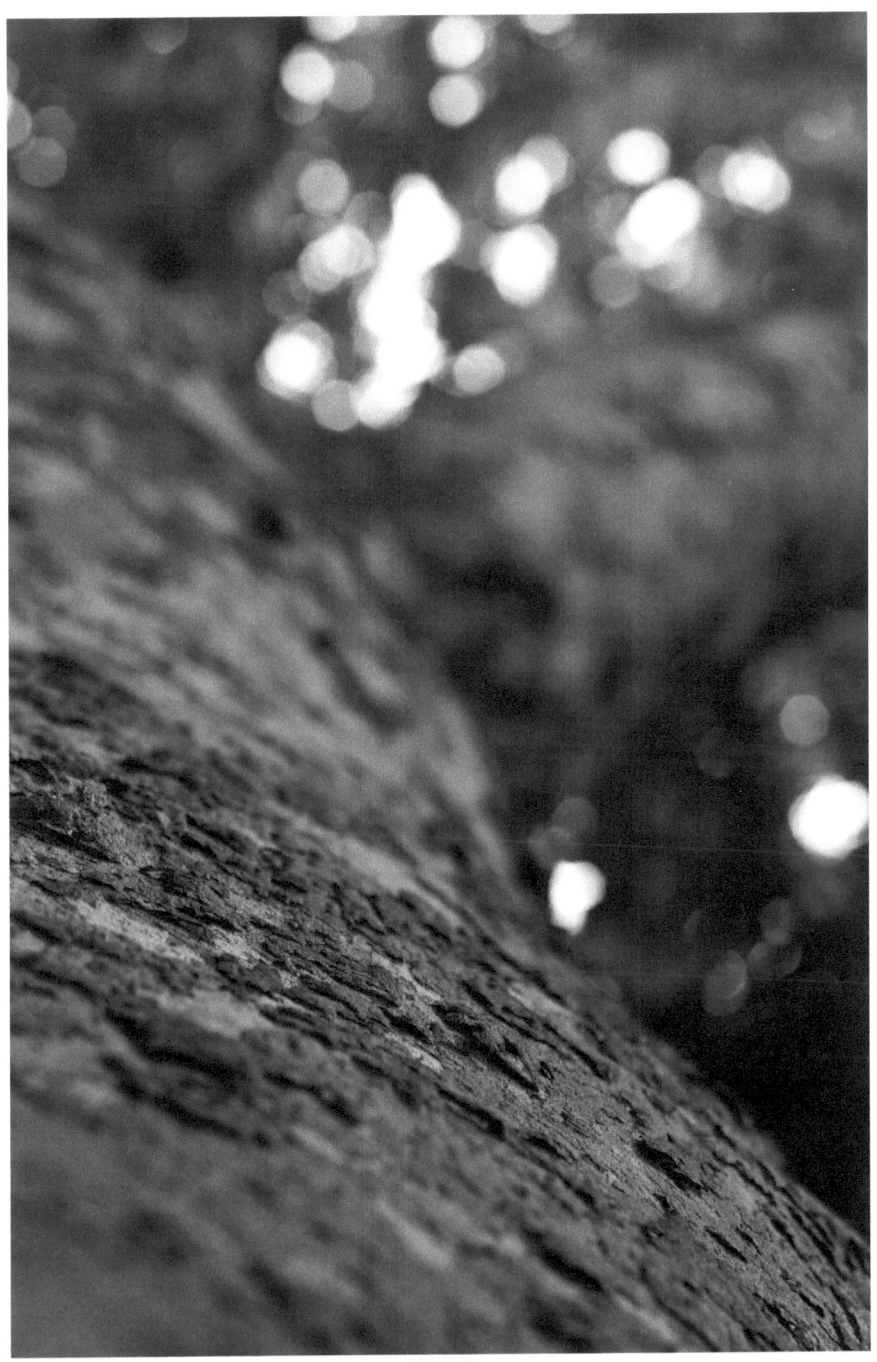

2068

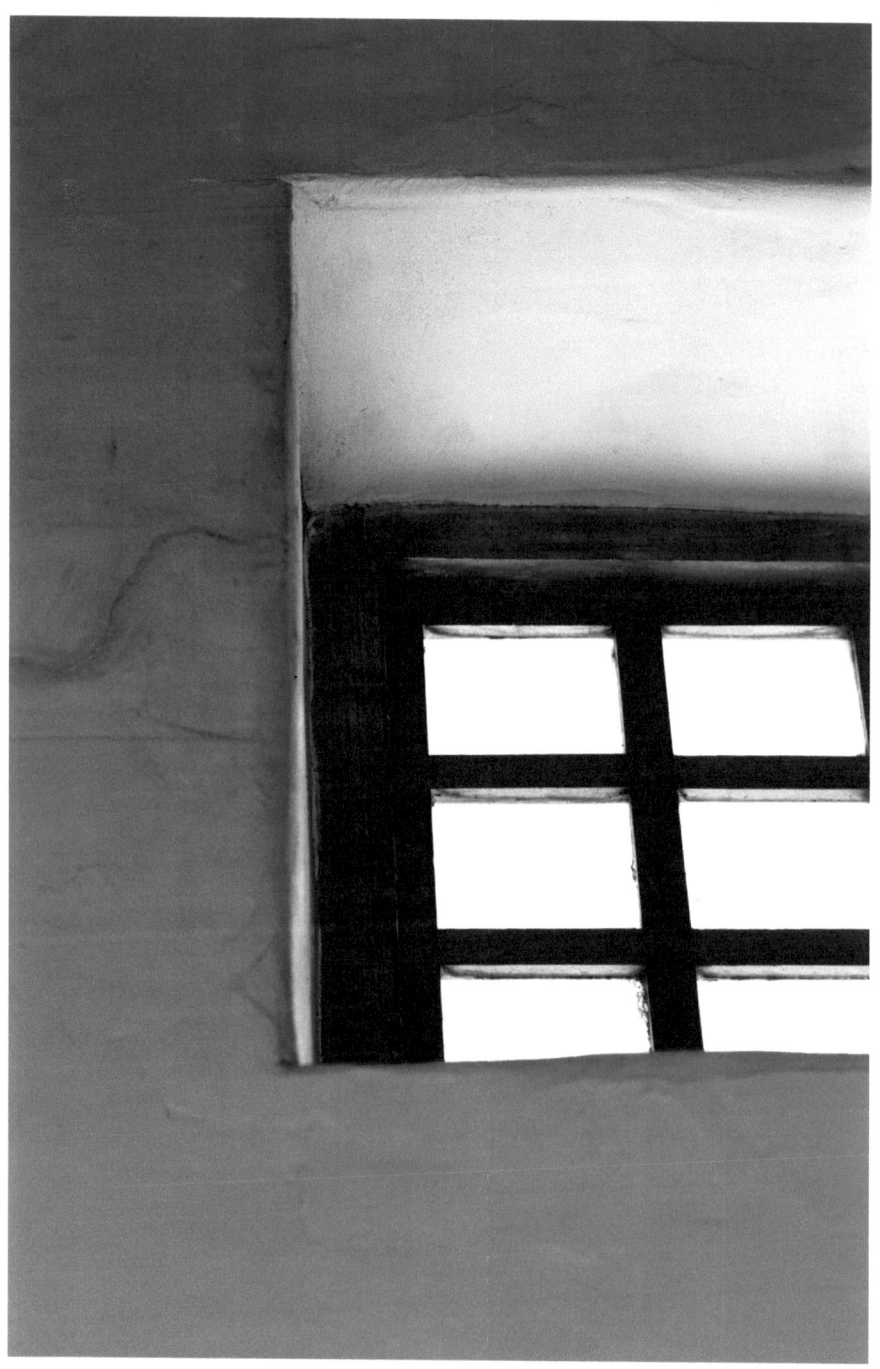

2397

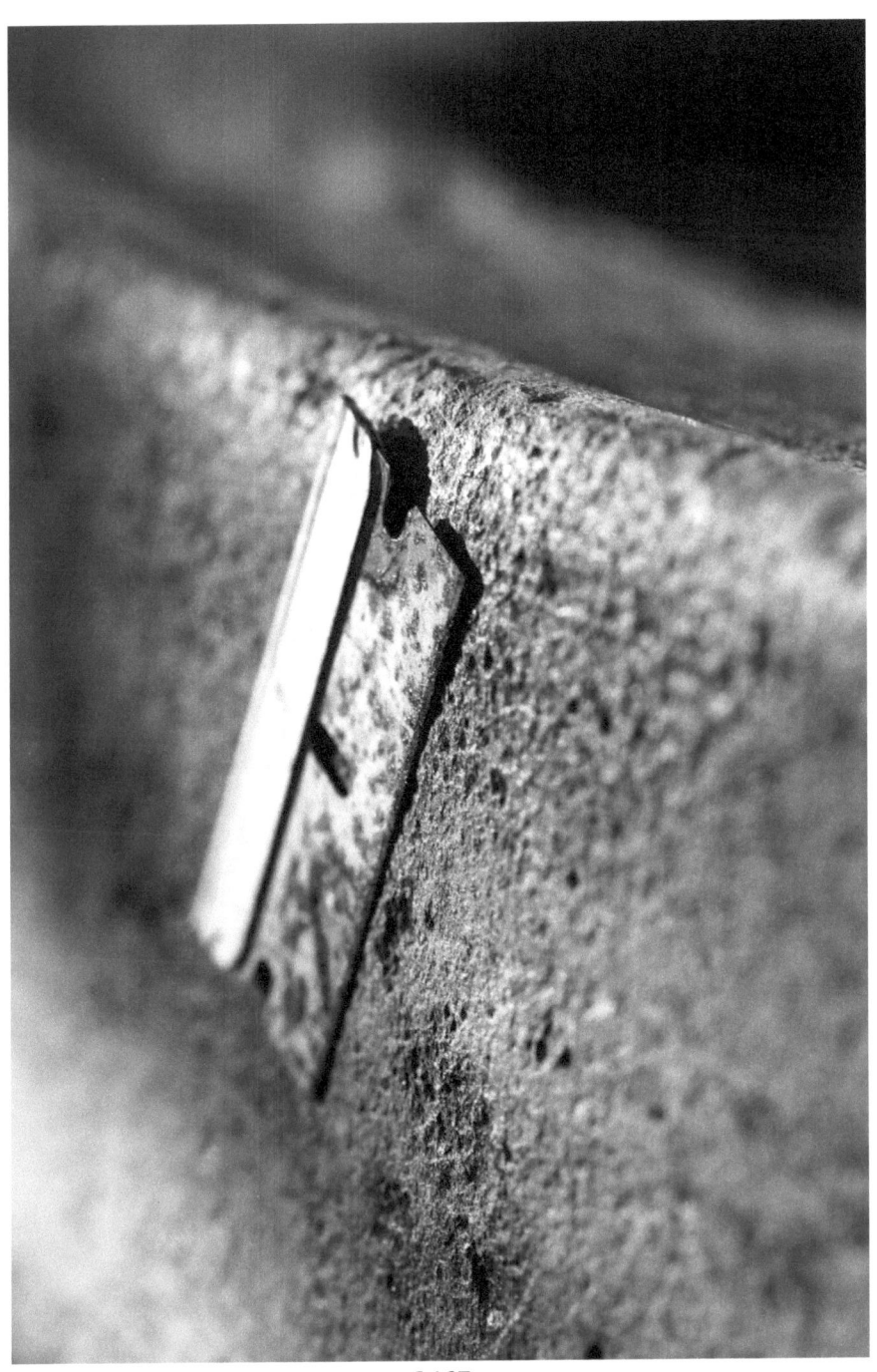

2467

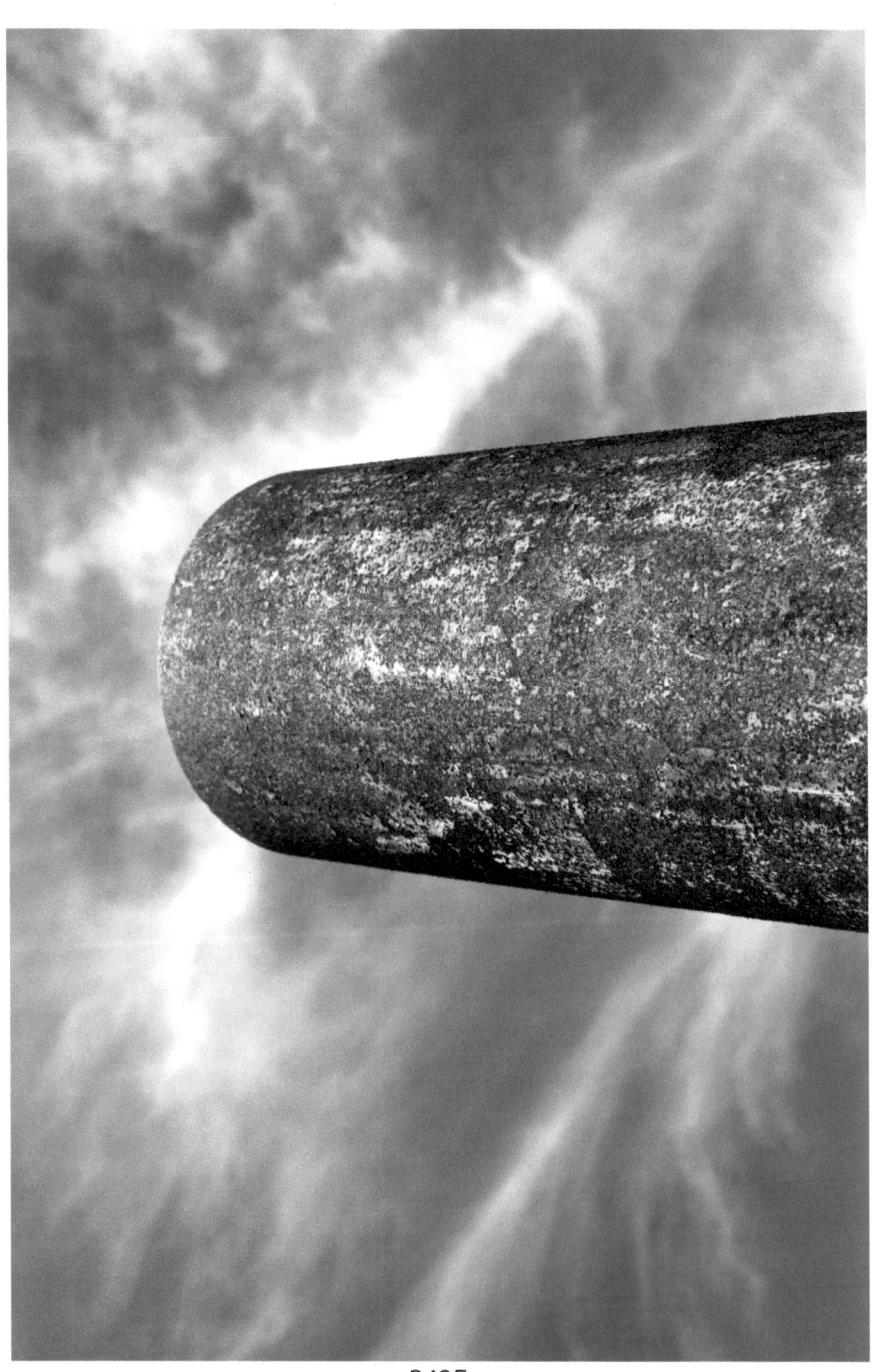

2495

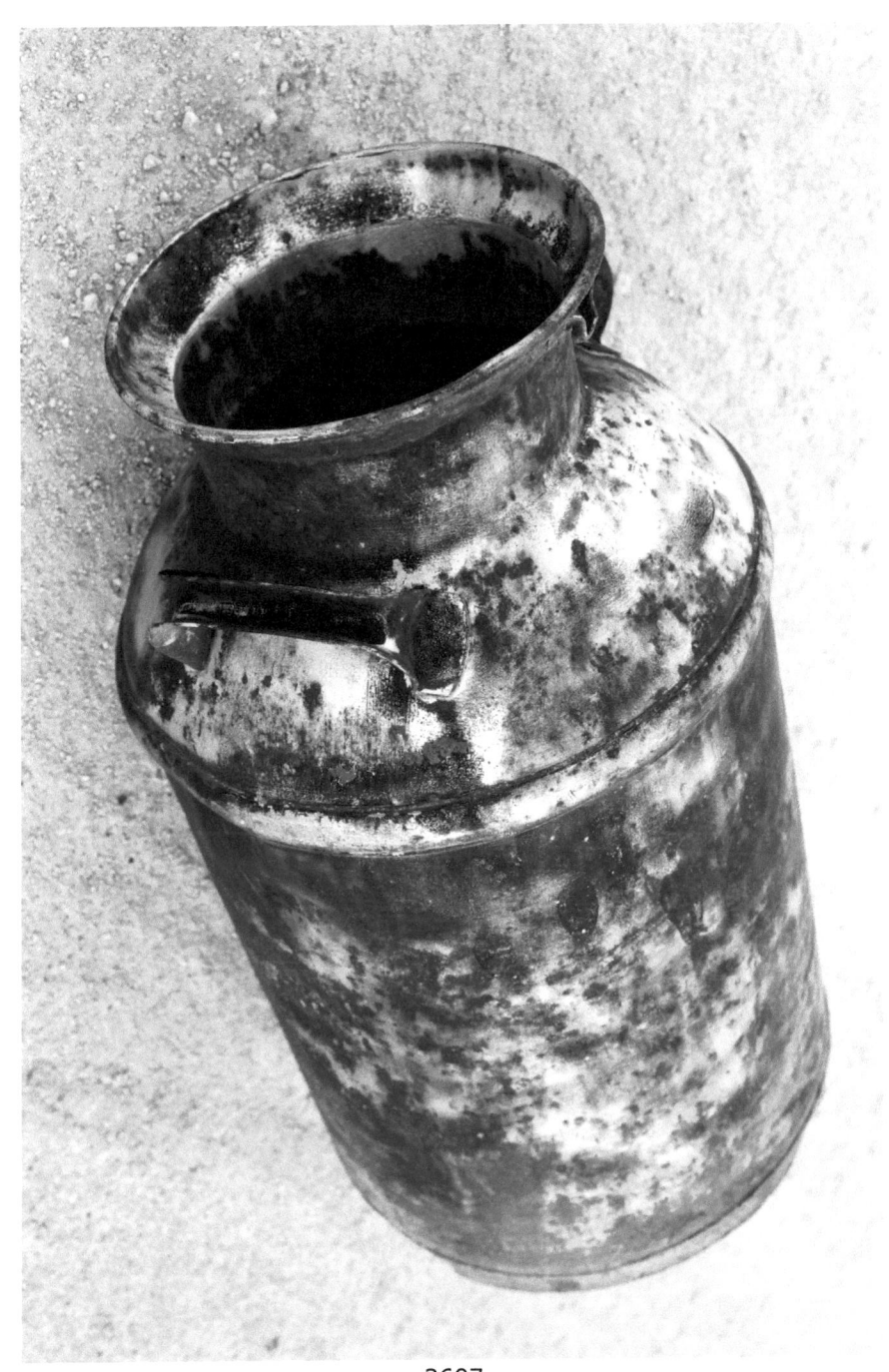

2607

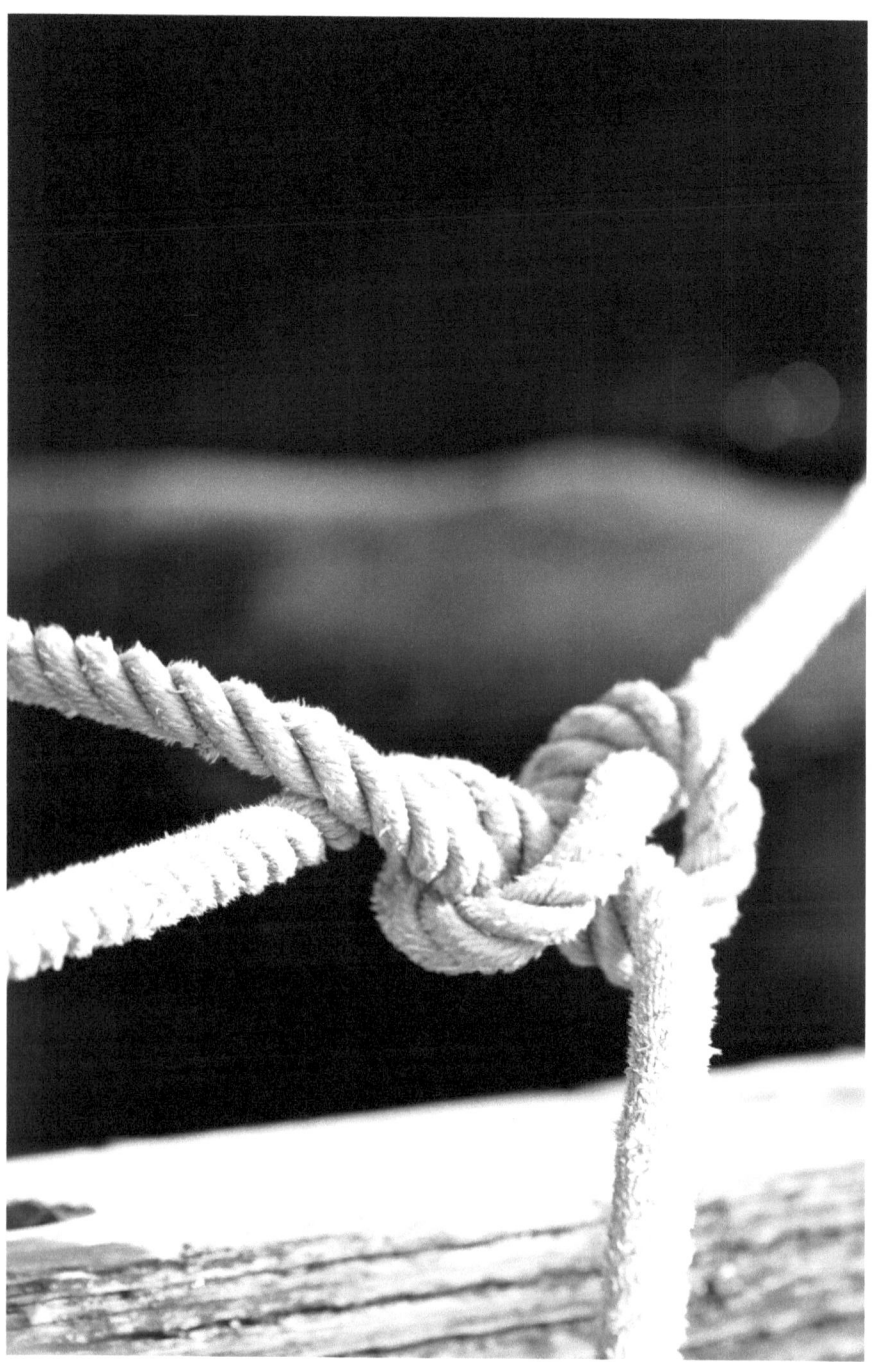

2686

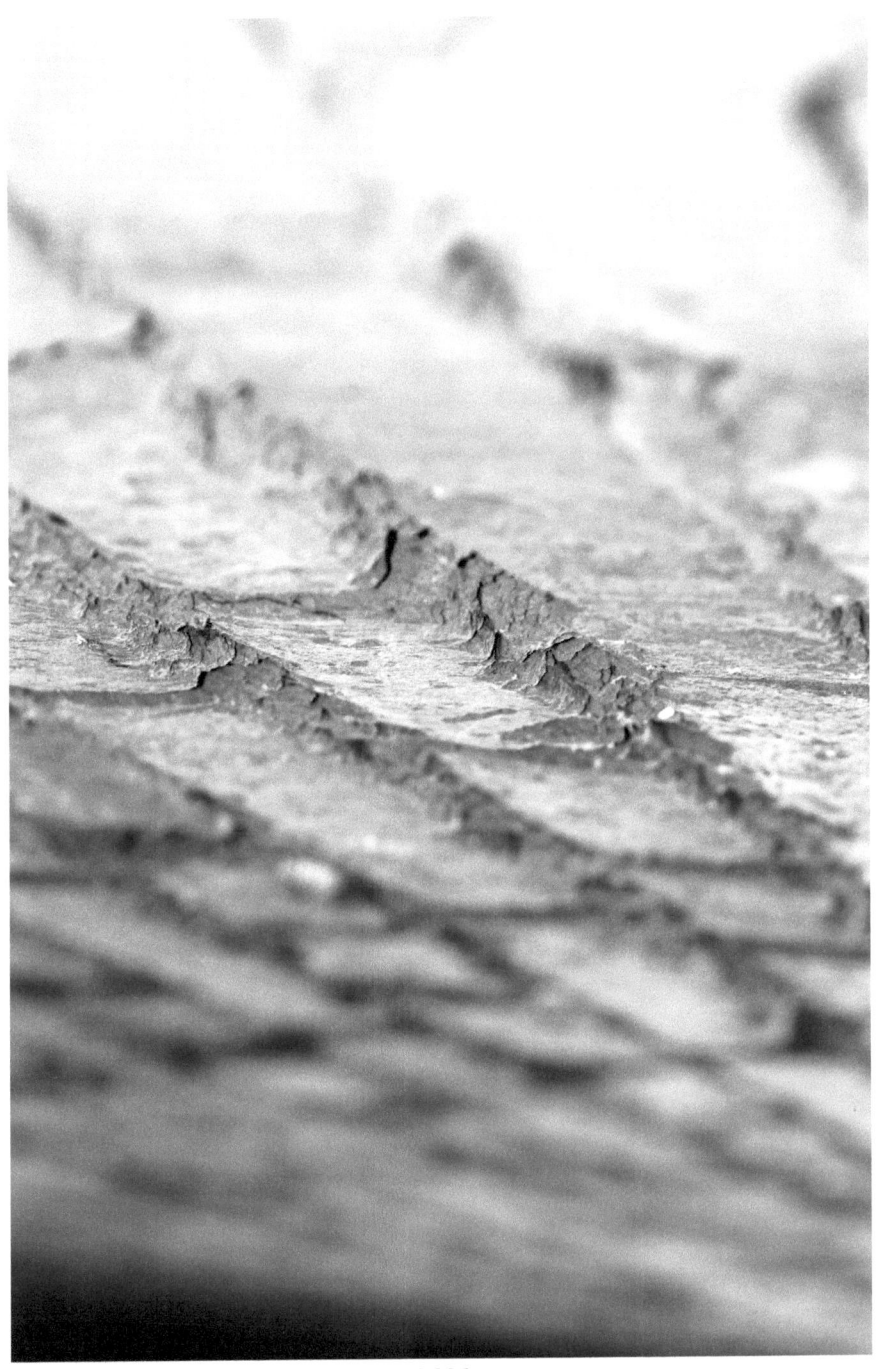

2688

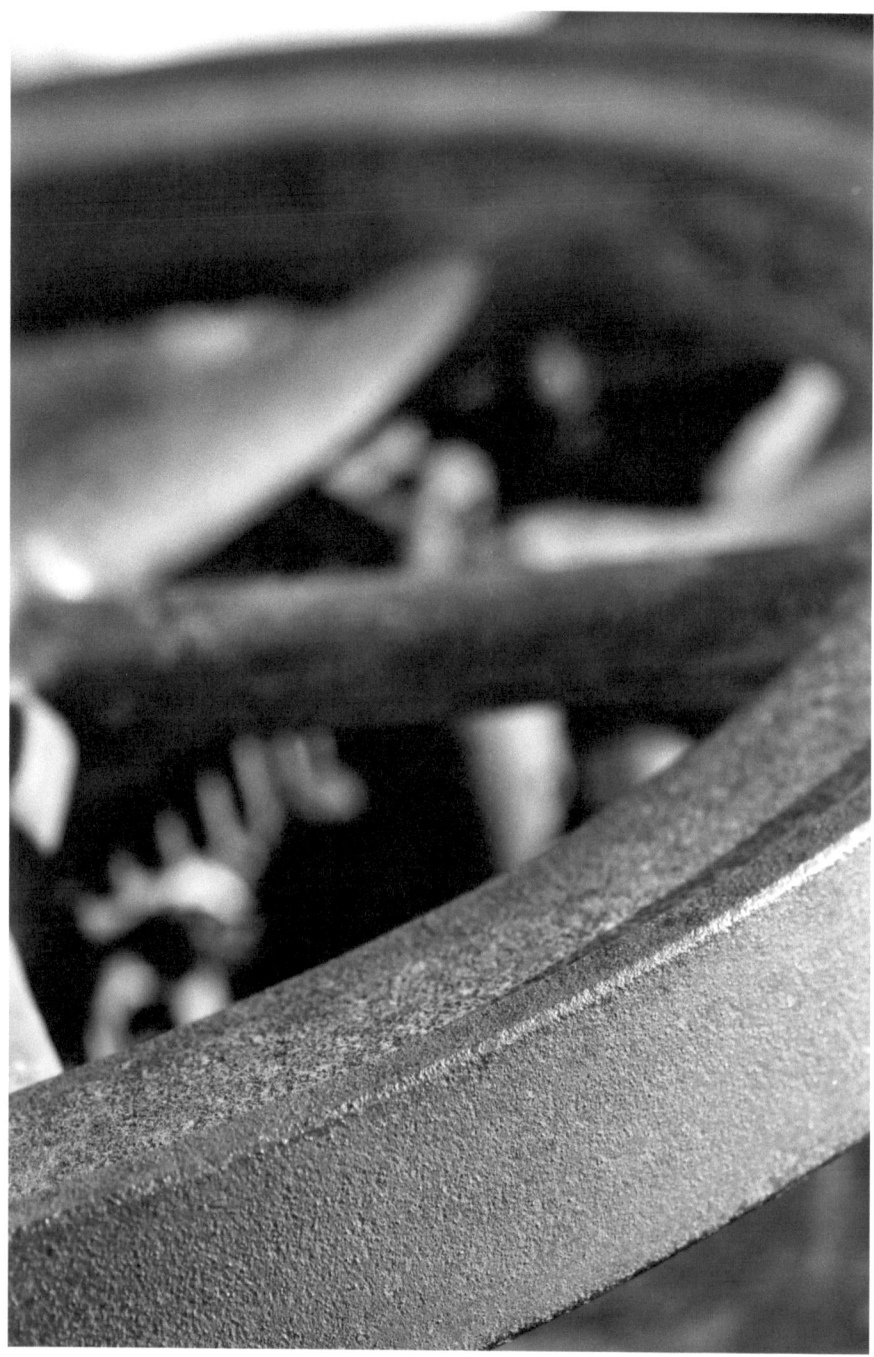

2962

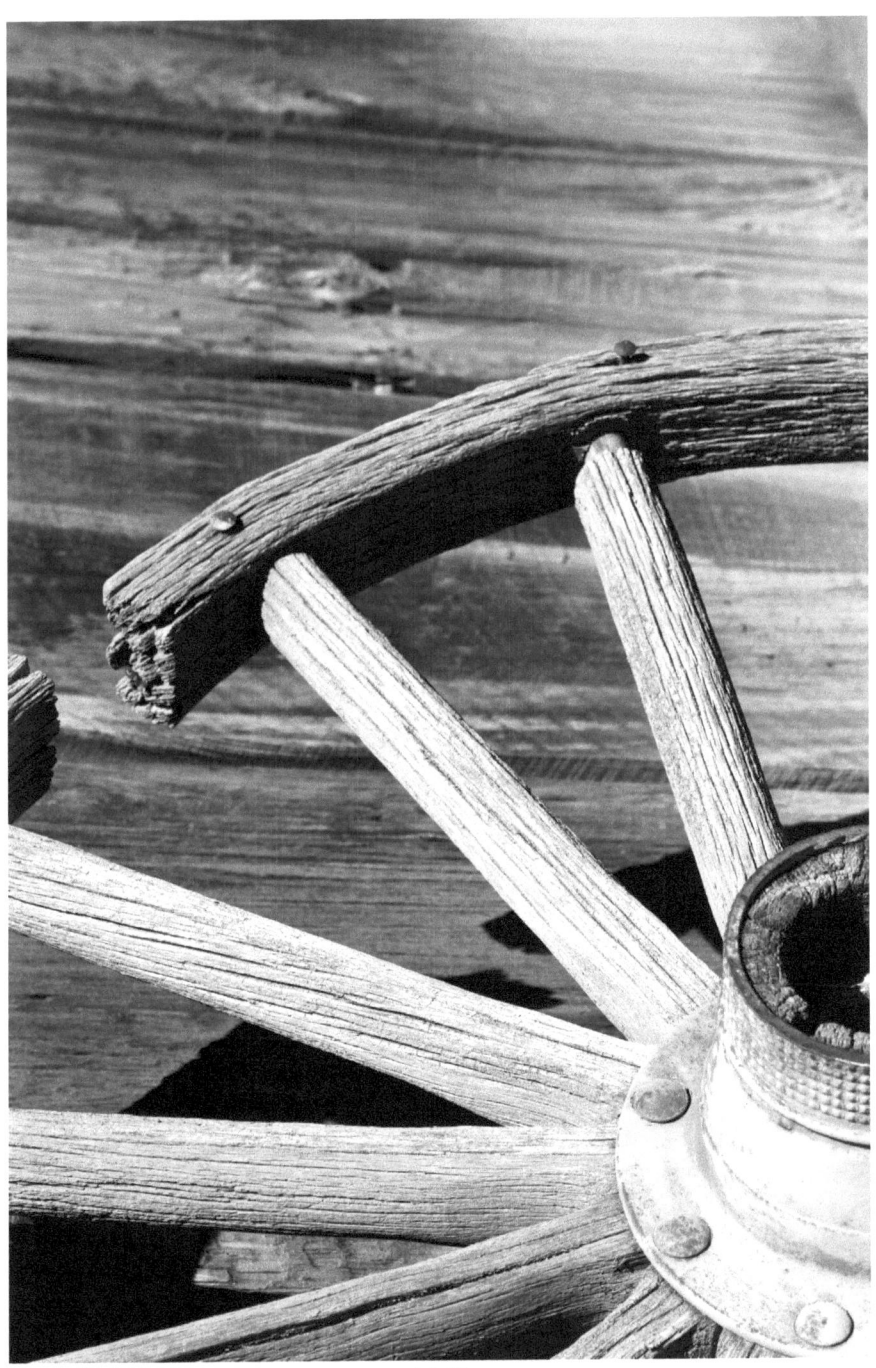

3147

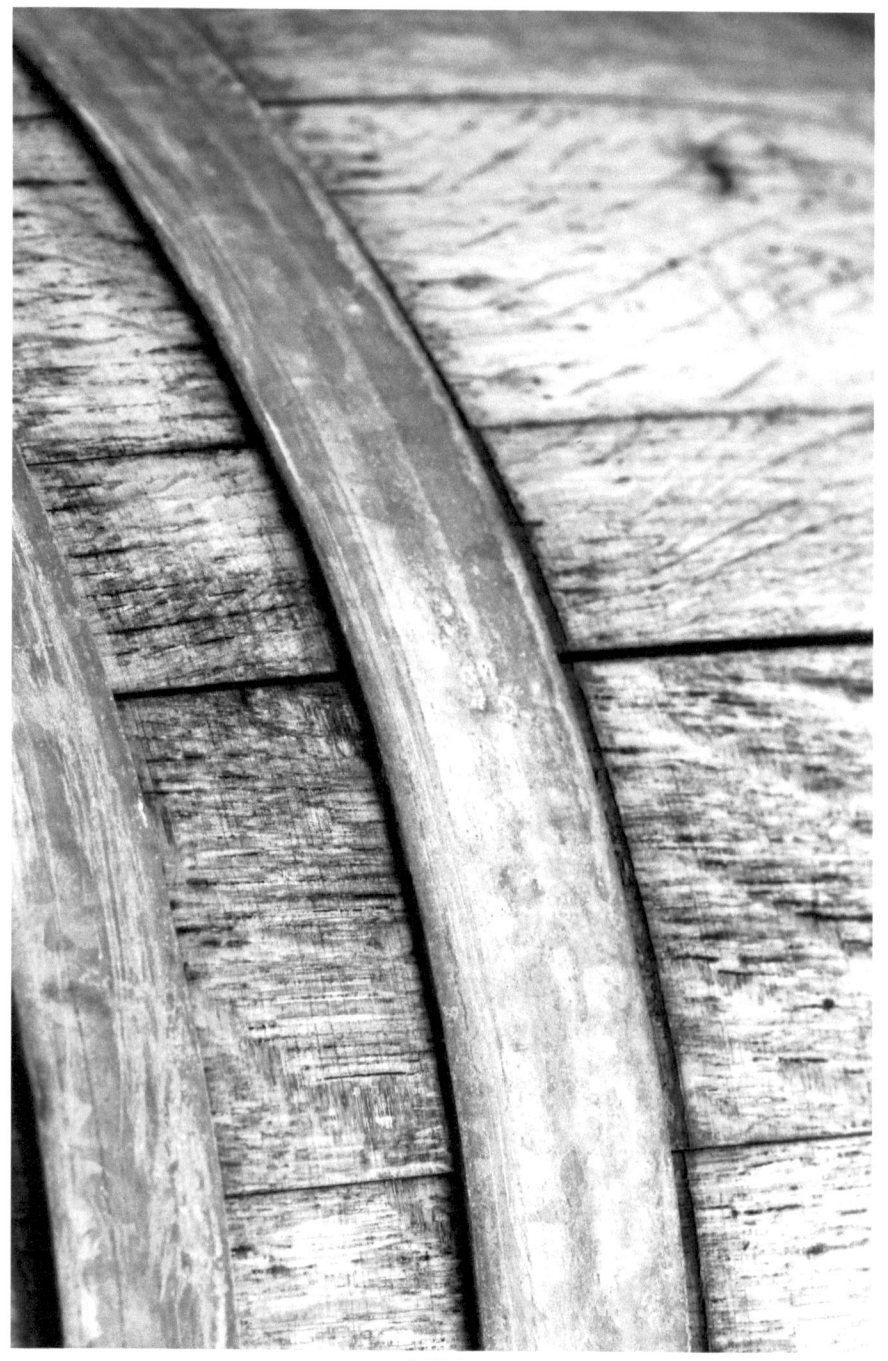

3151

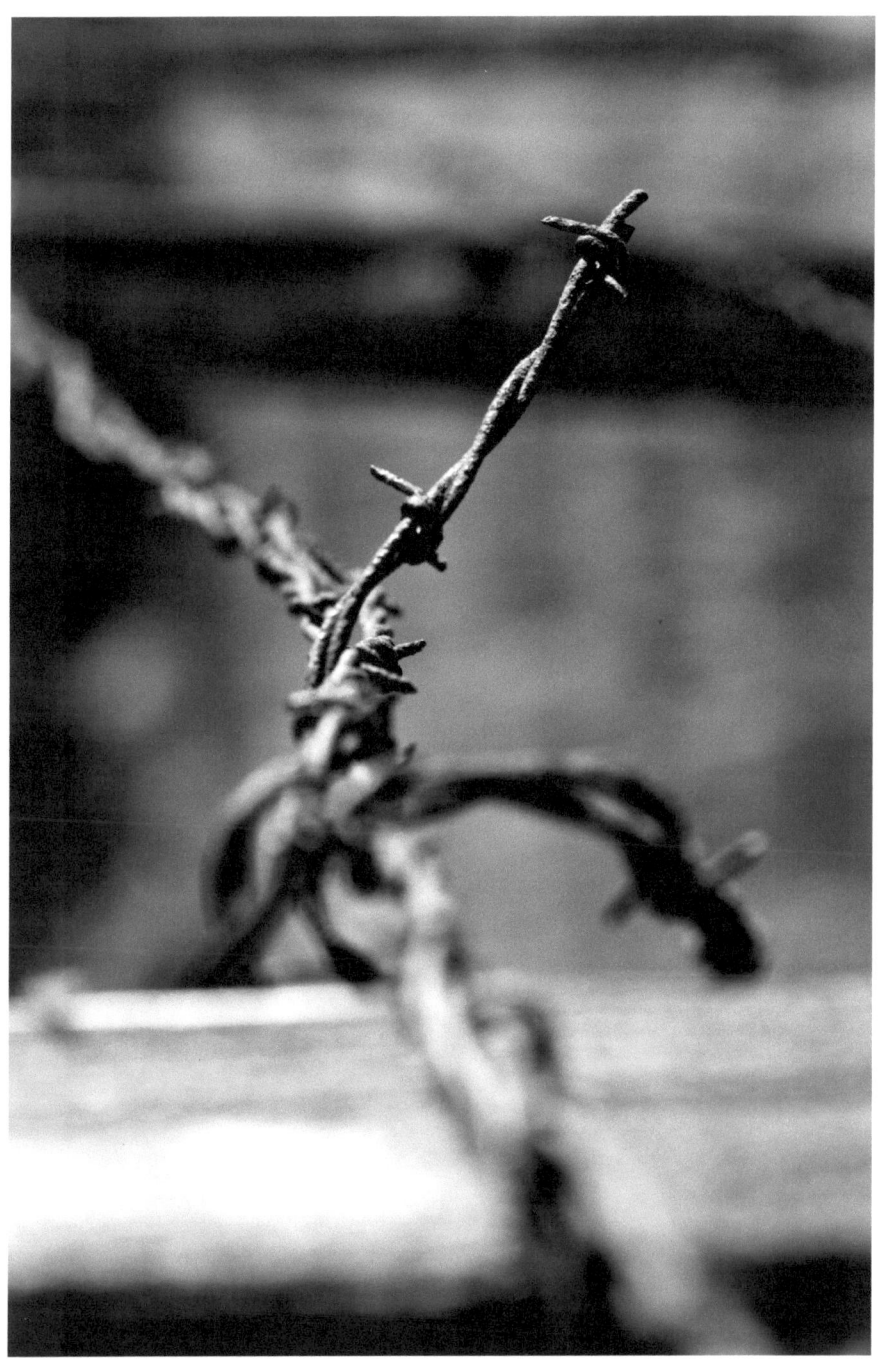

3359

3621

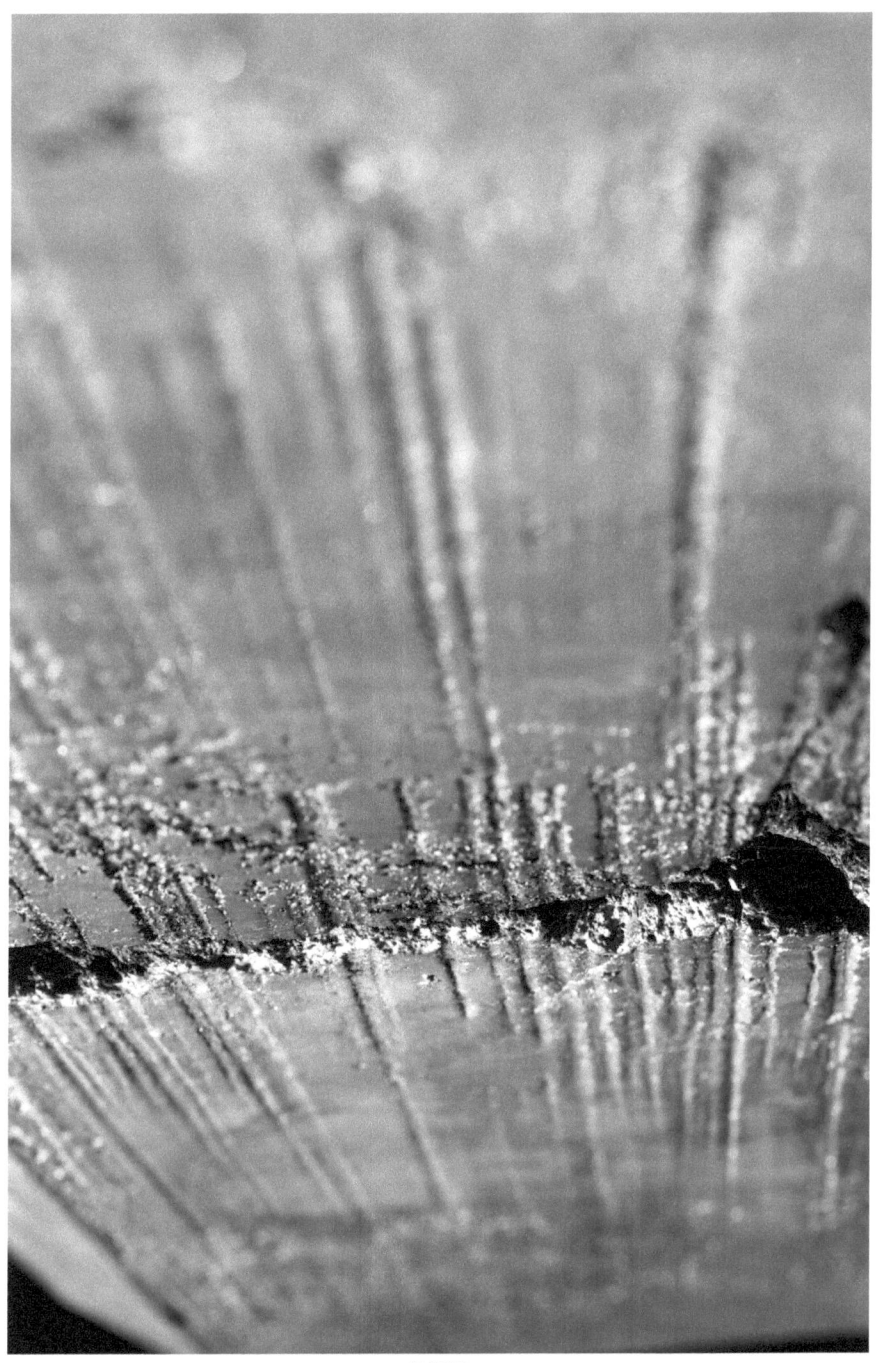

3656

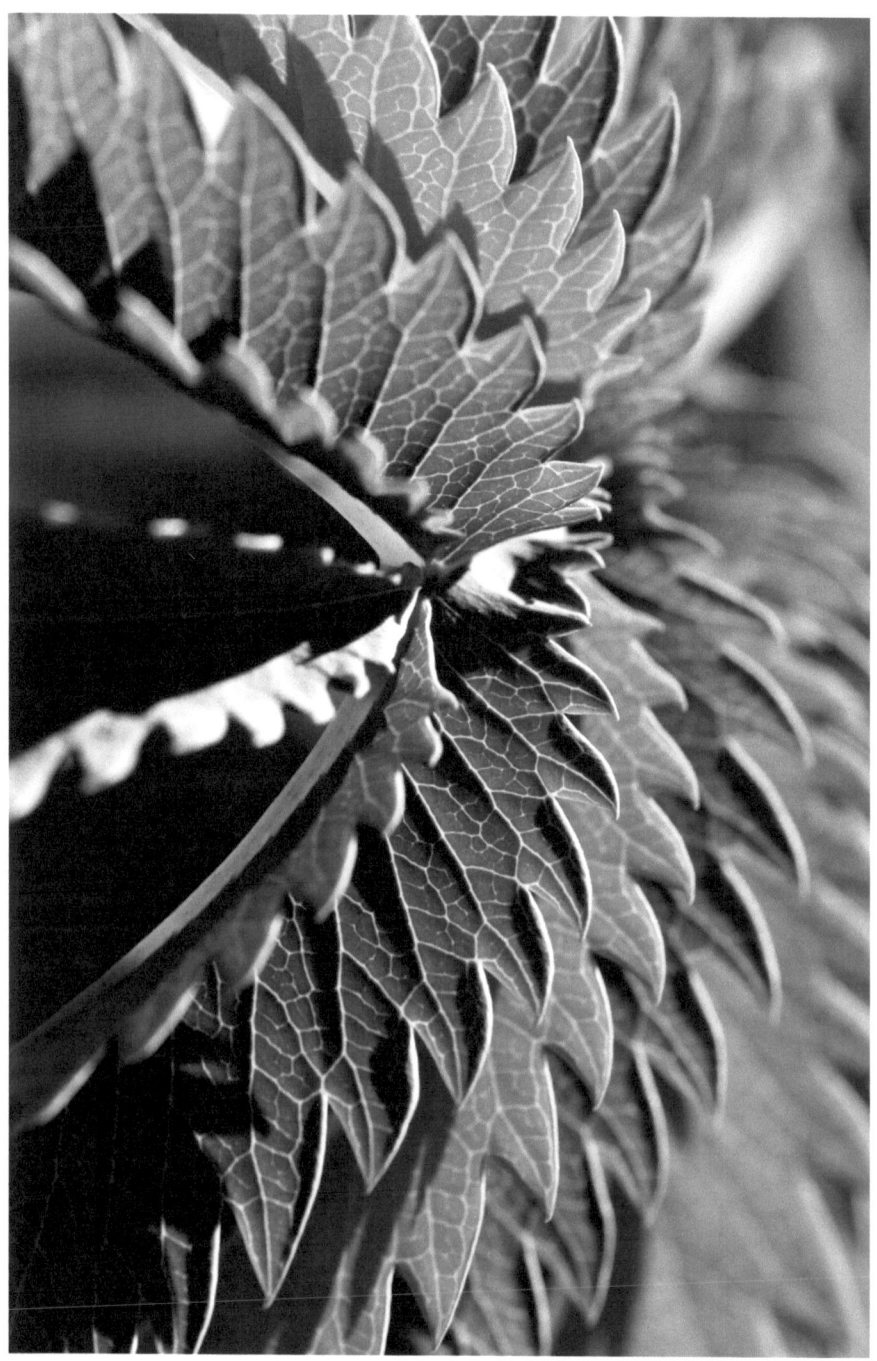

3714

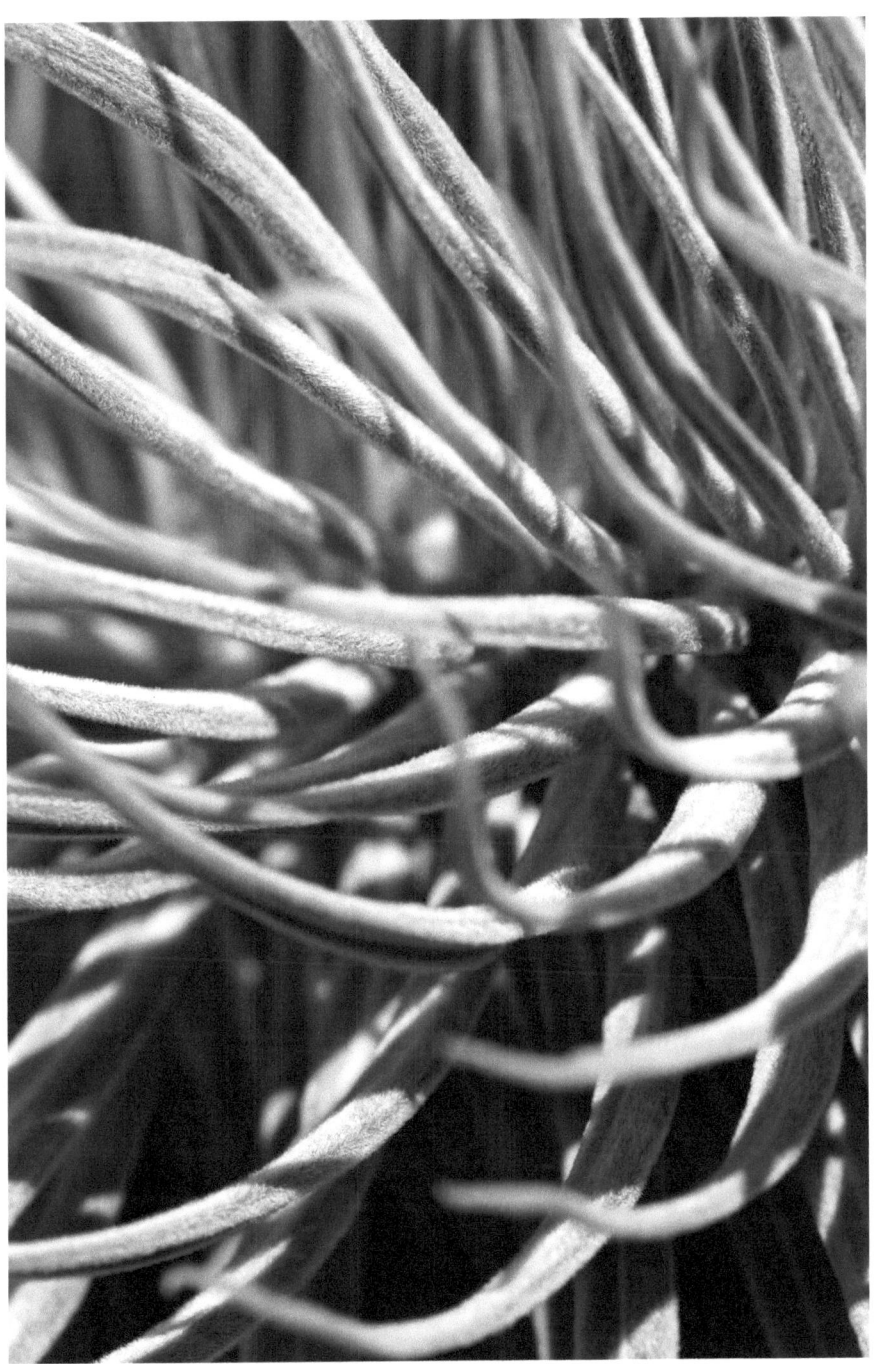

3752

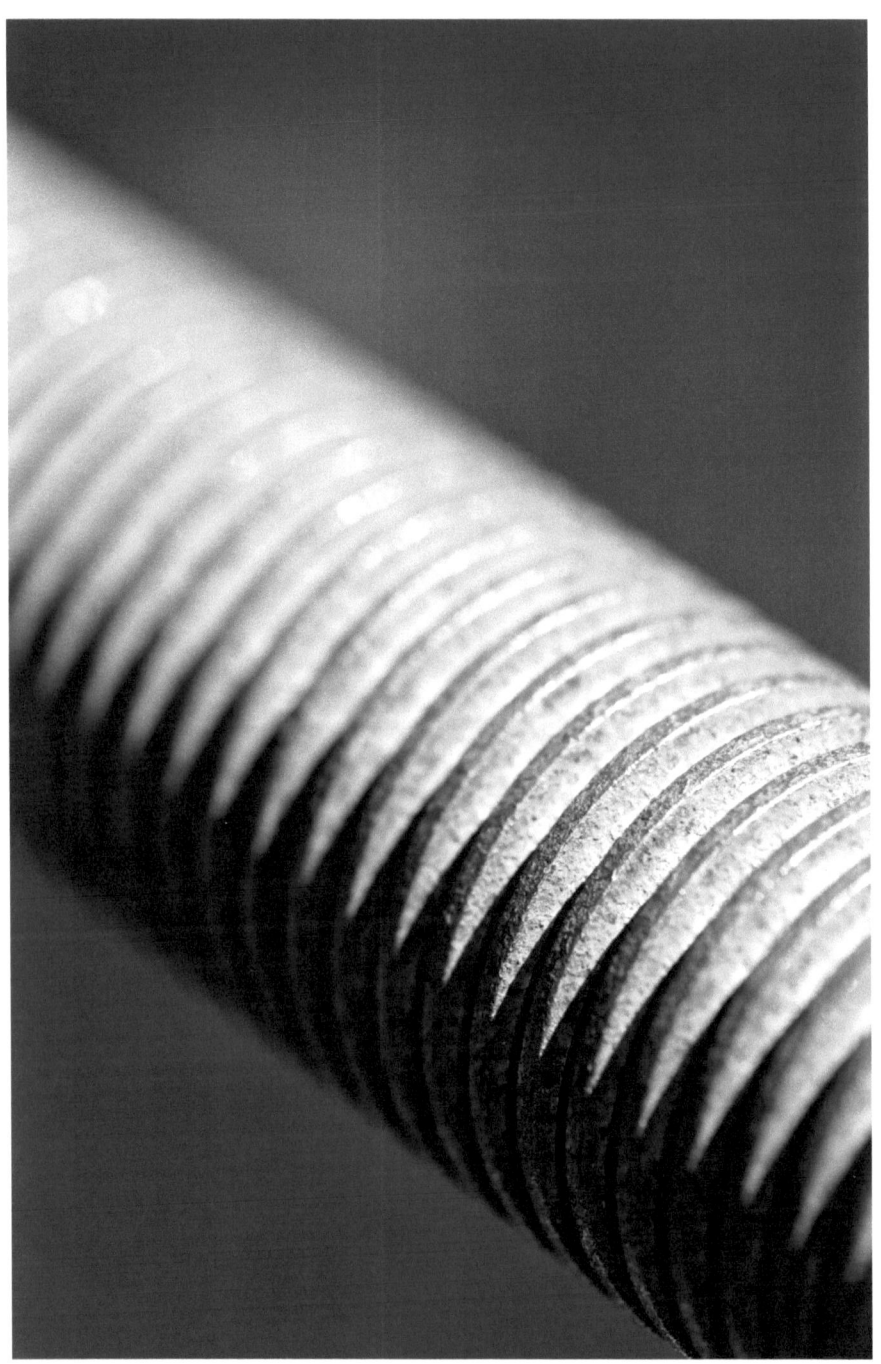

3937

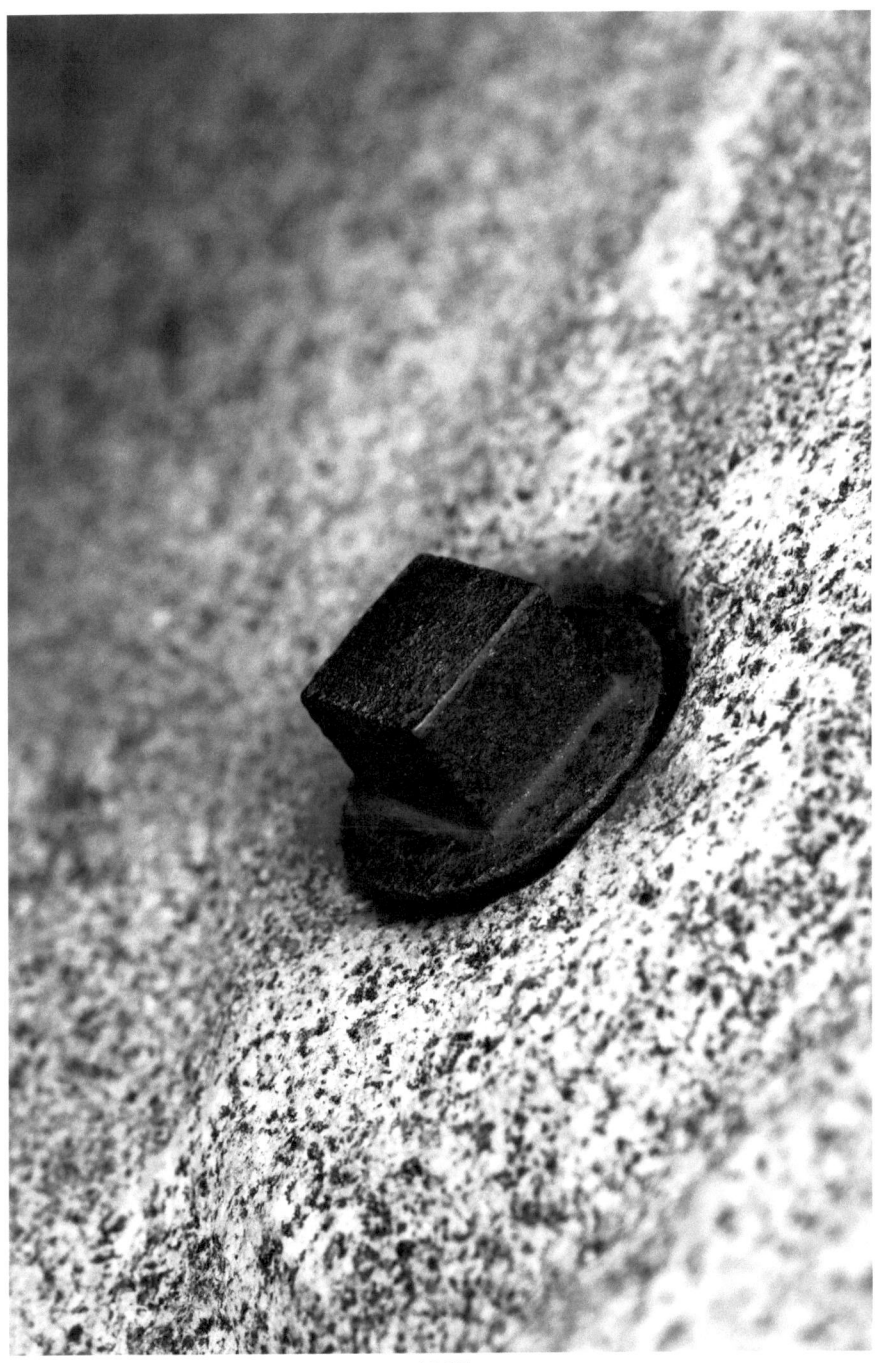

4035

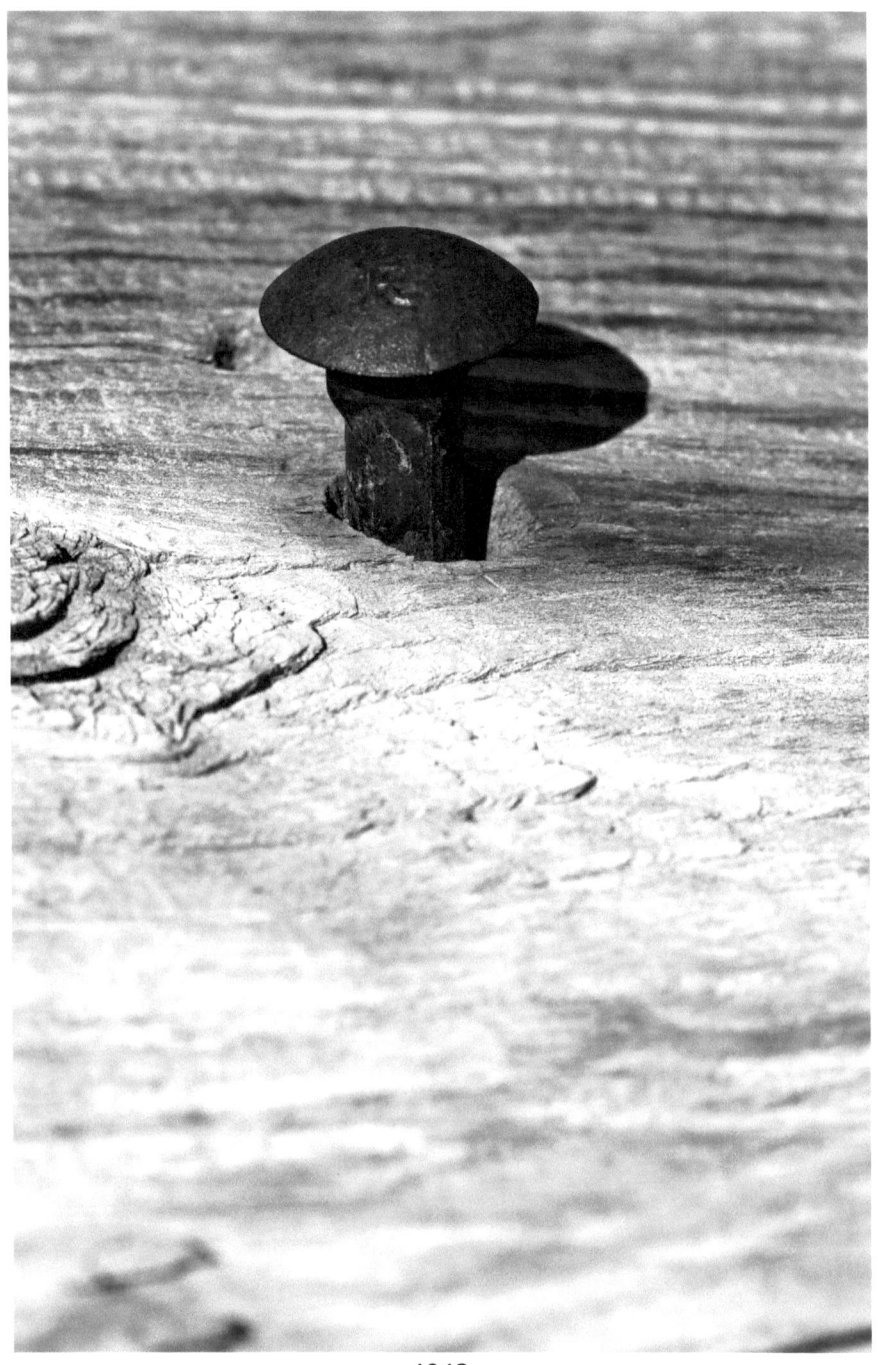

4043

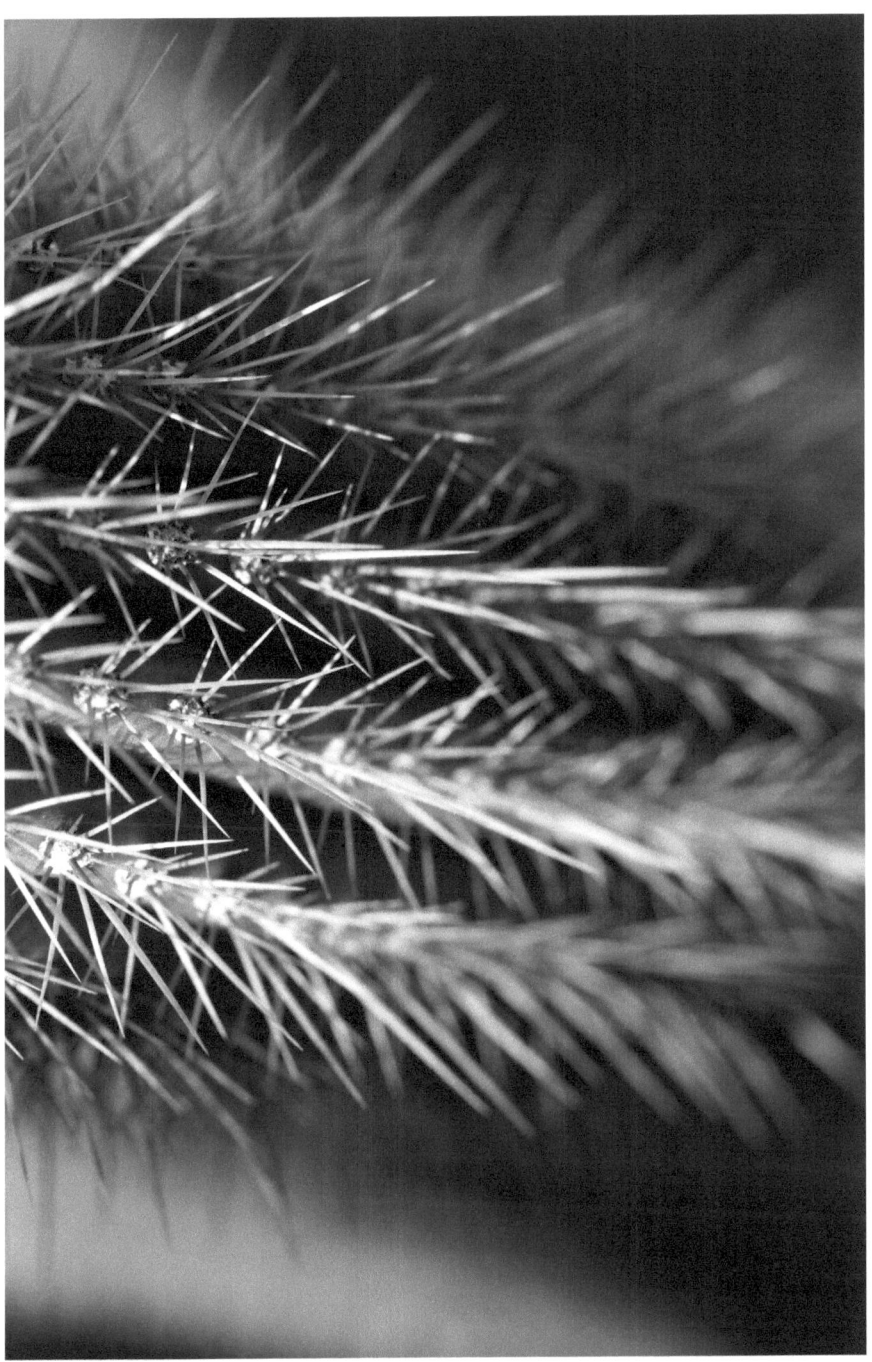

4070

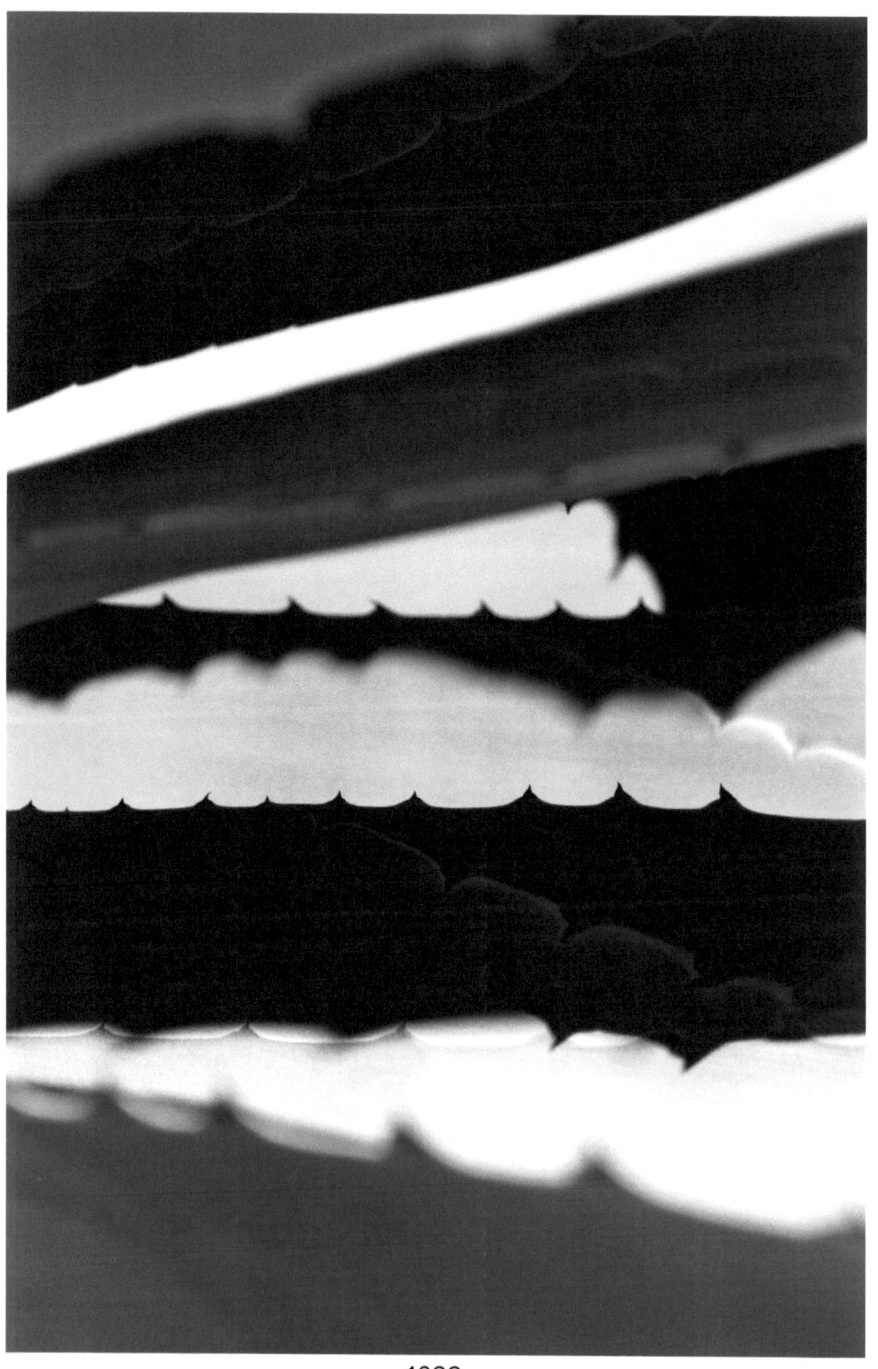

4099

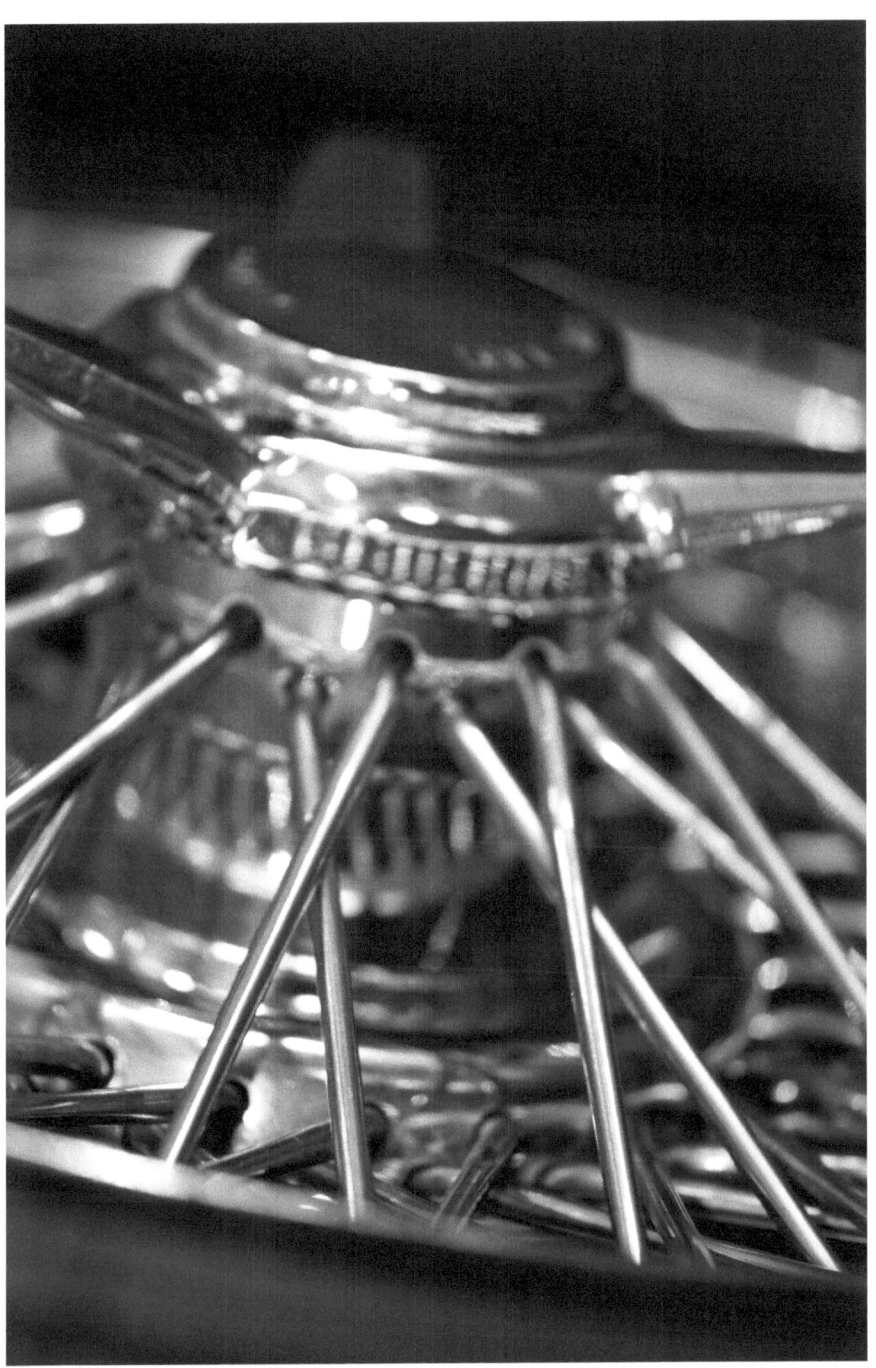

4193

5171

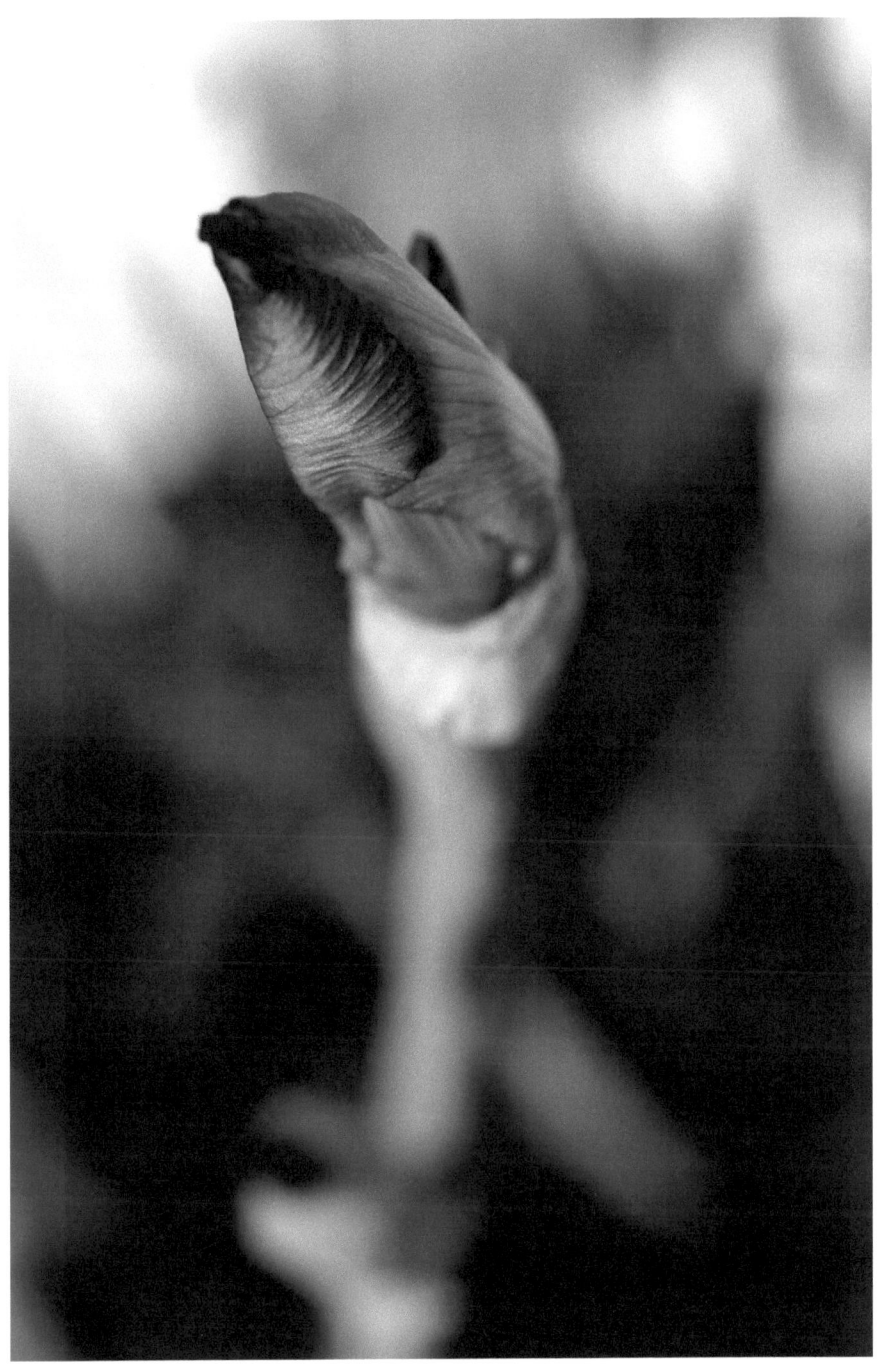

5492

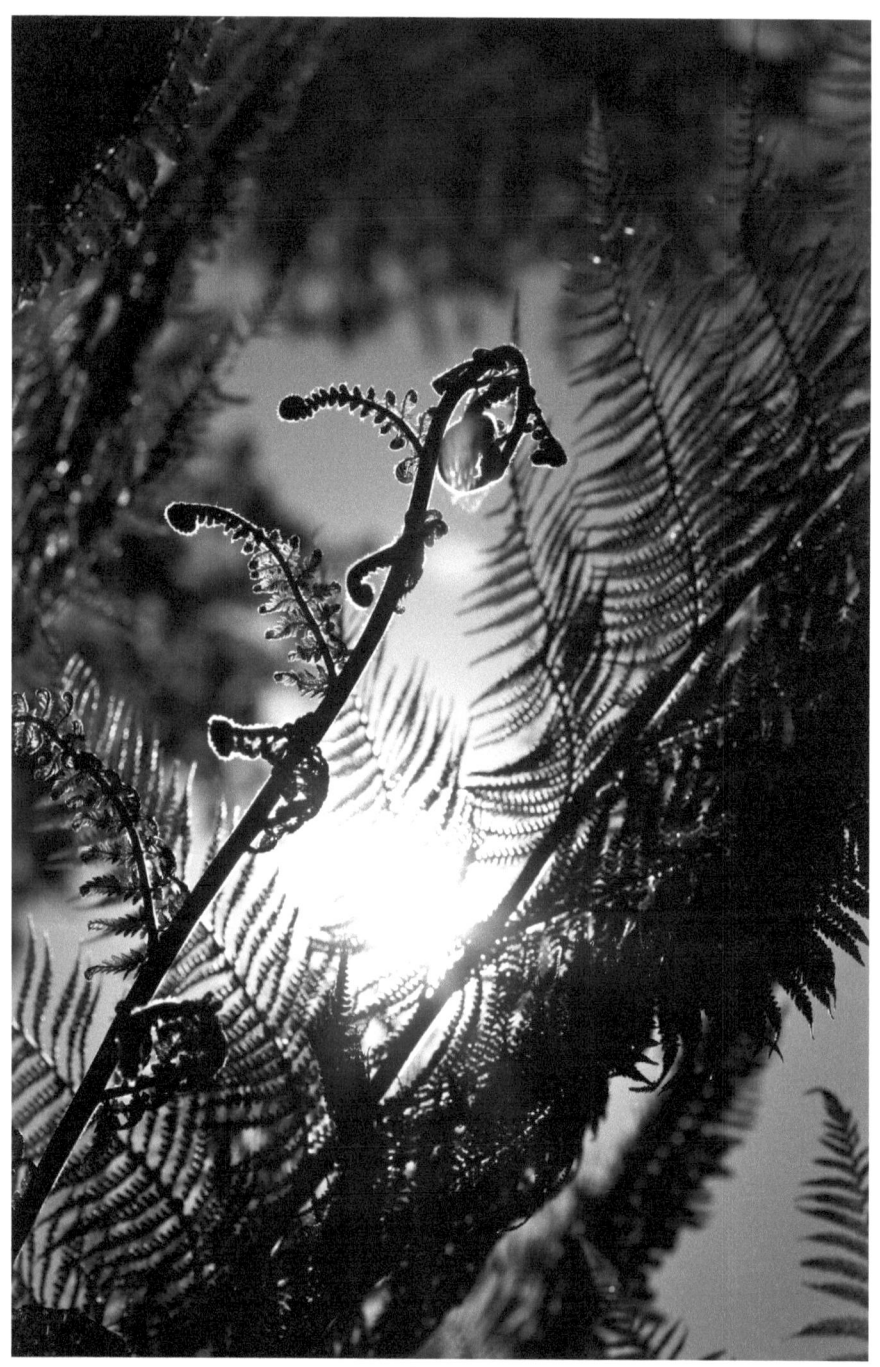

5705

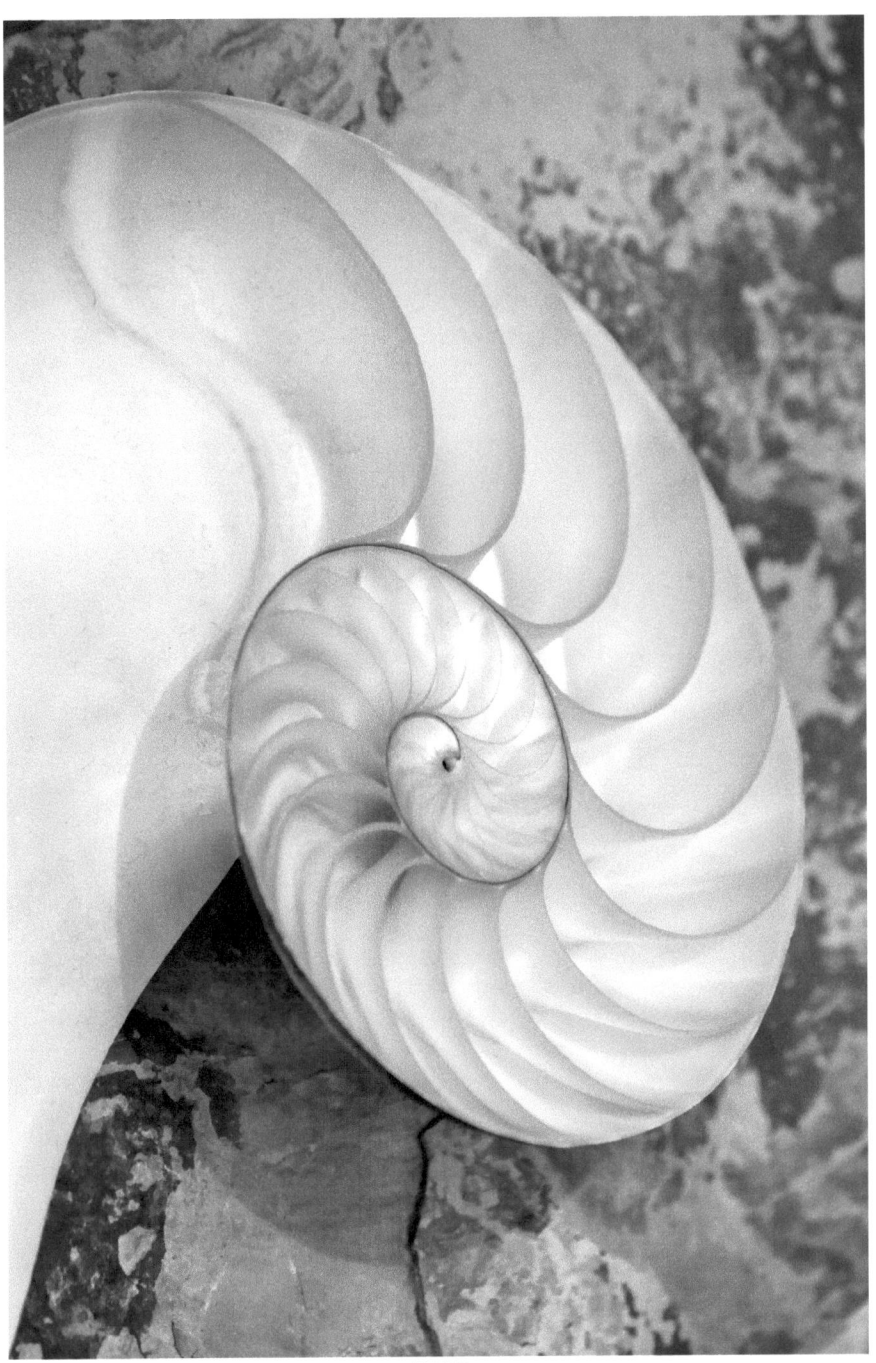

5708

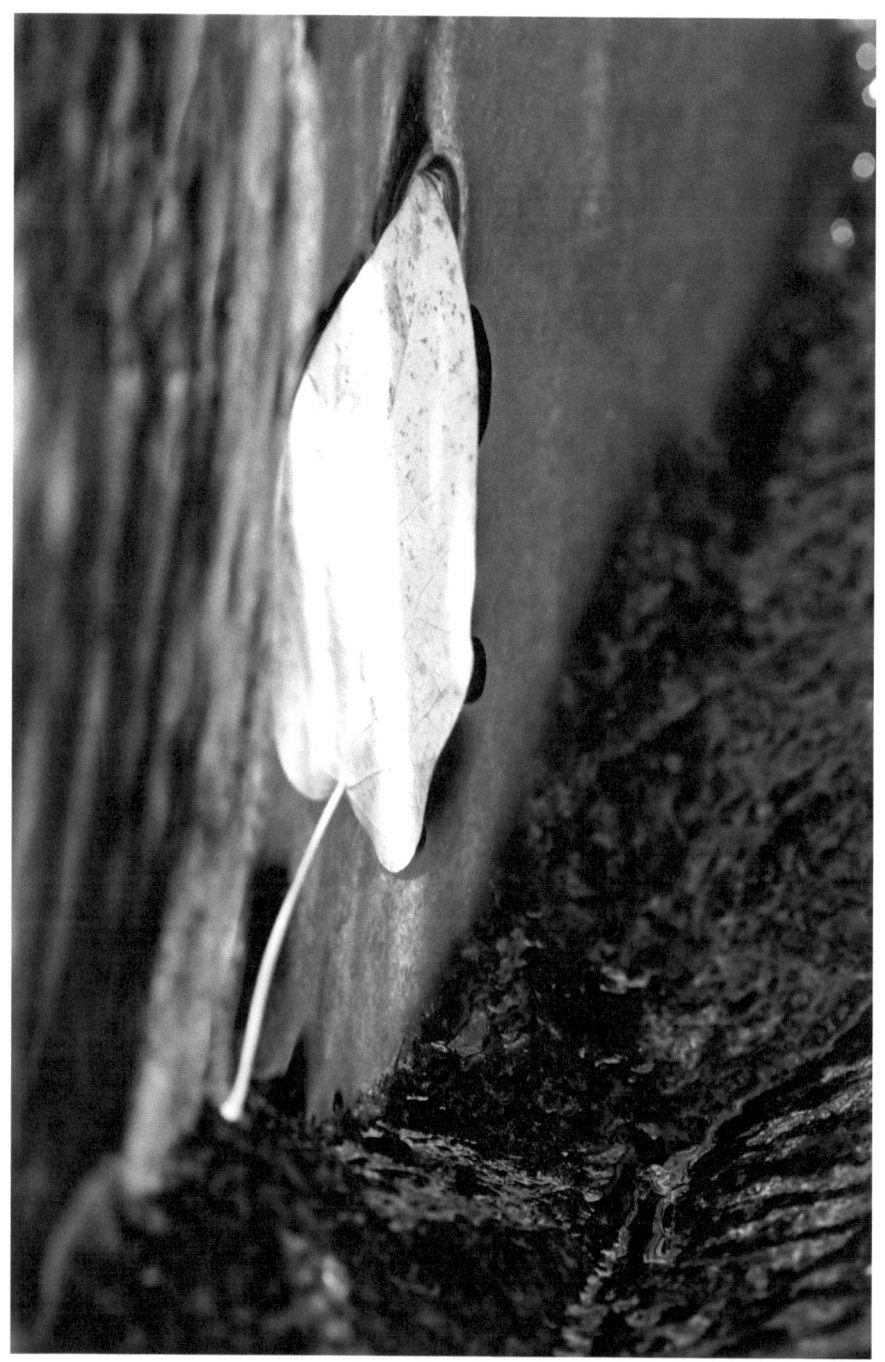

5750

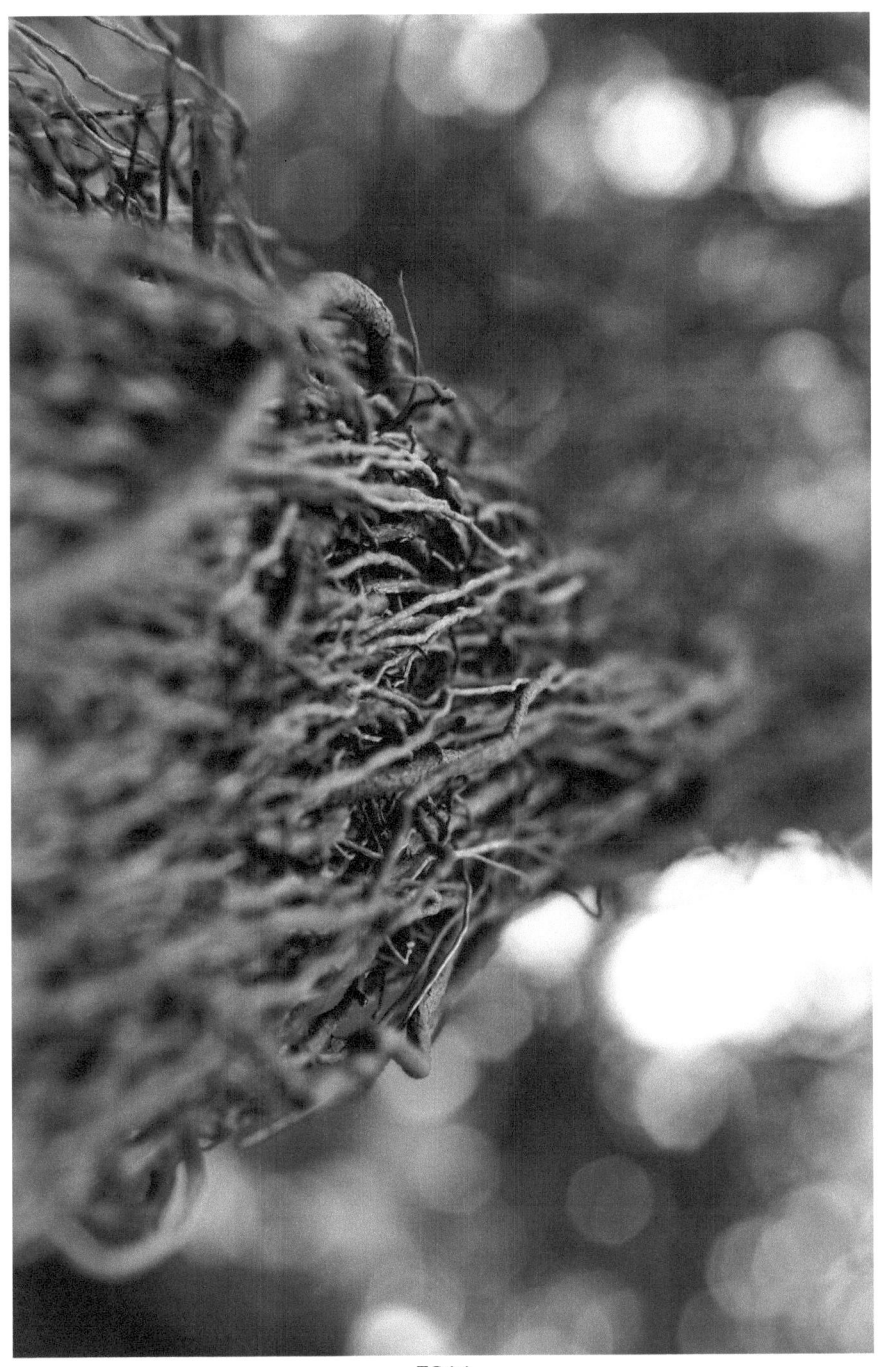

5811

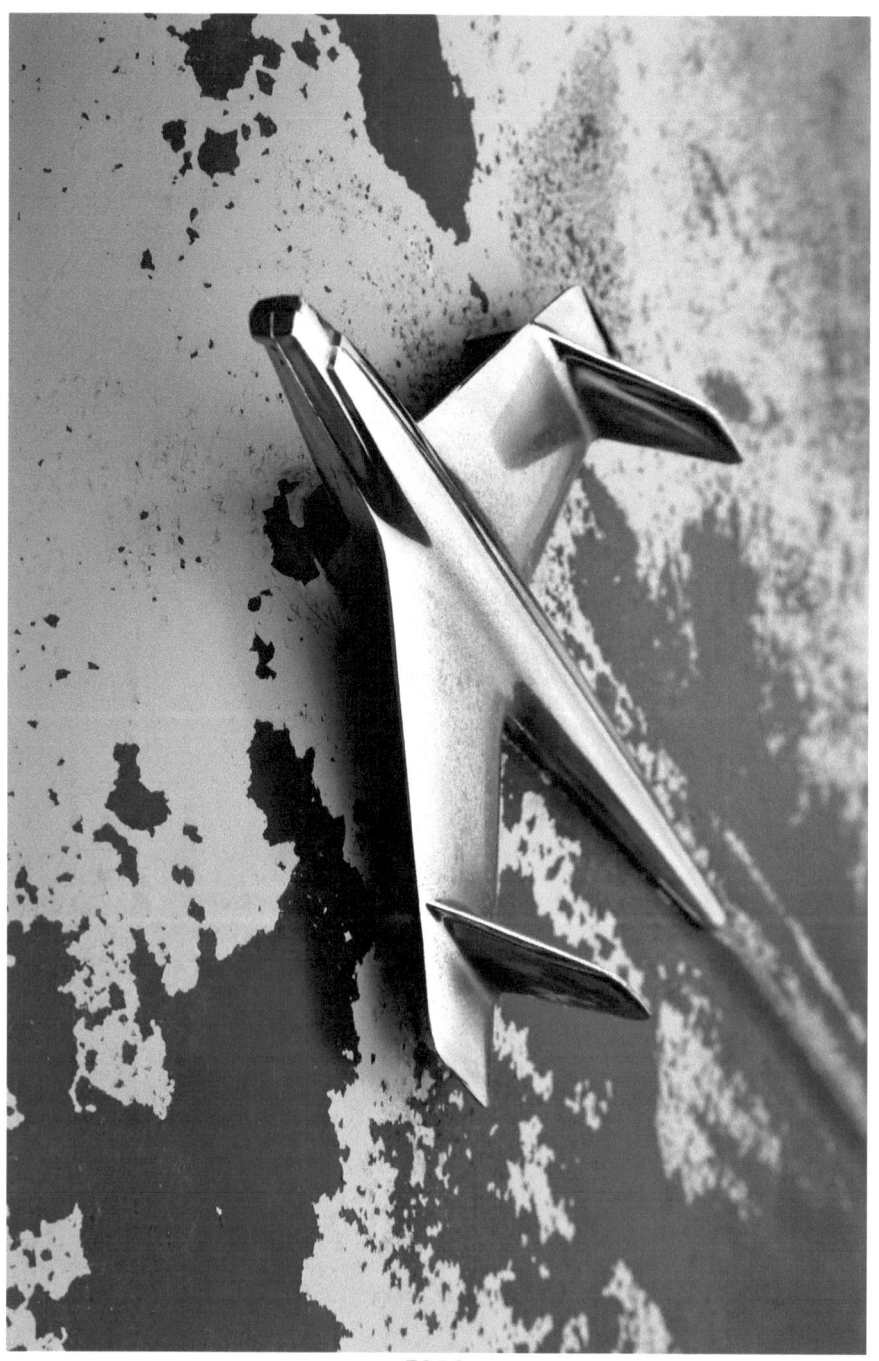

5846

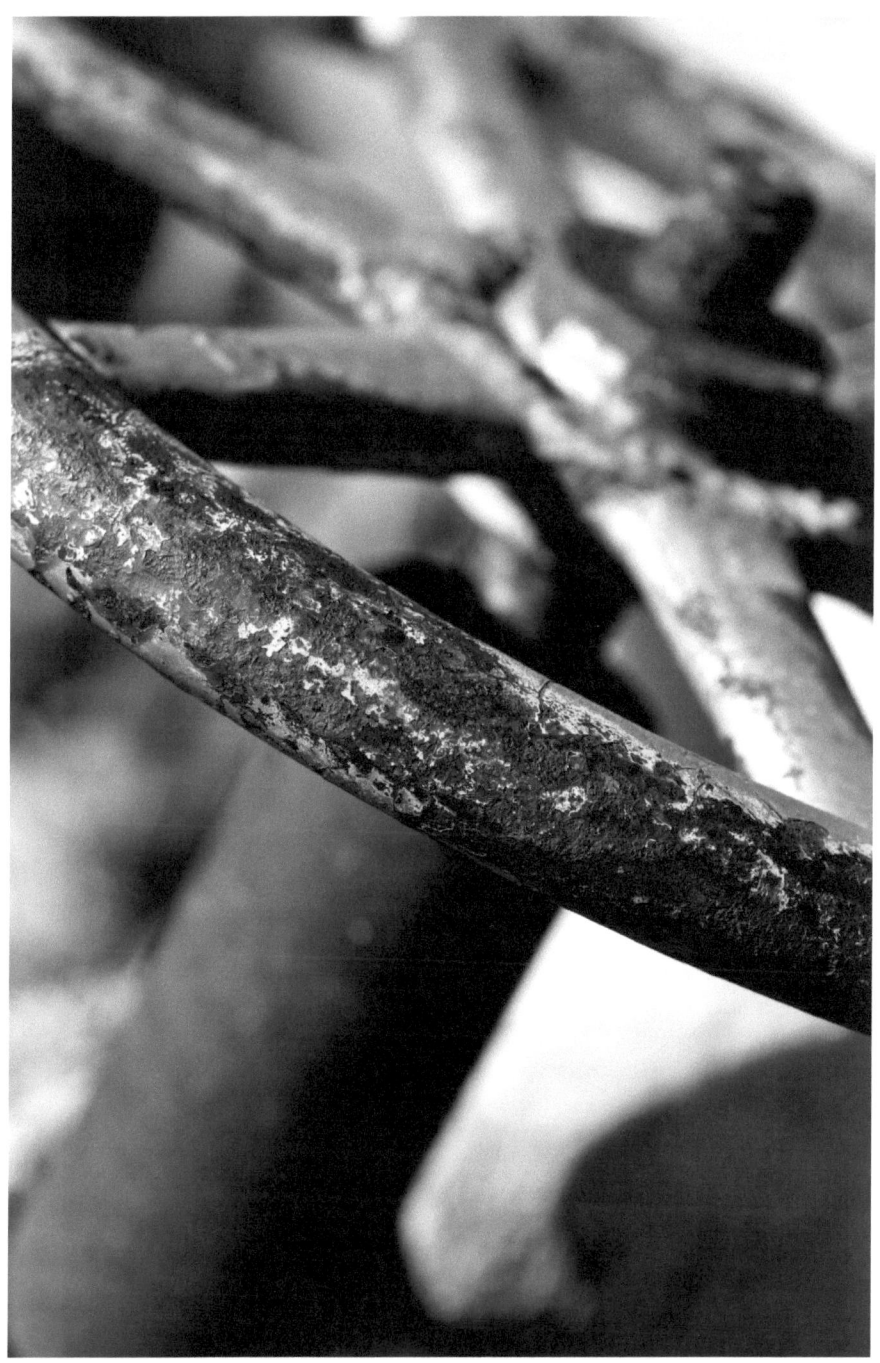

6095

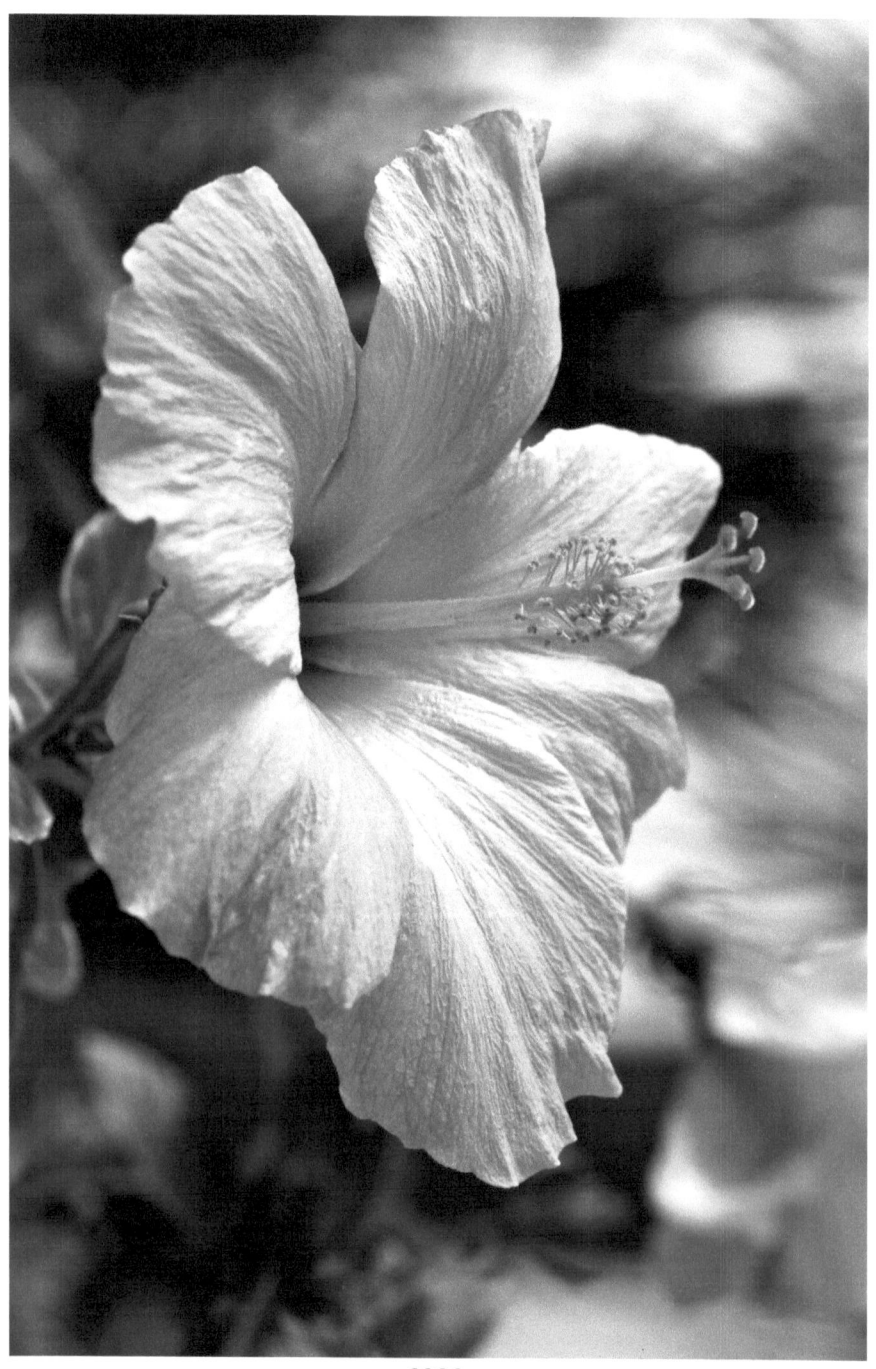

6990

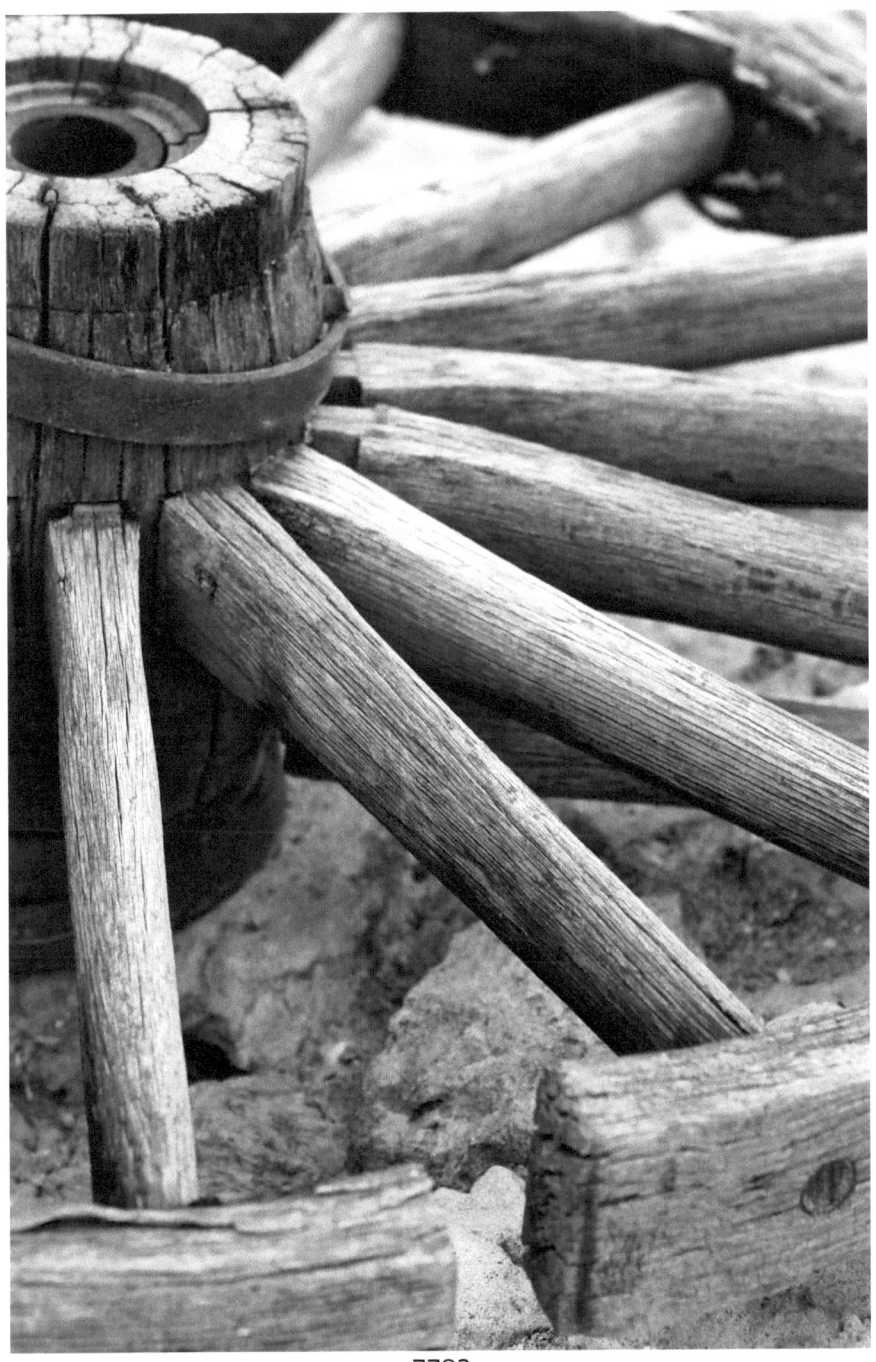

7783

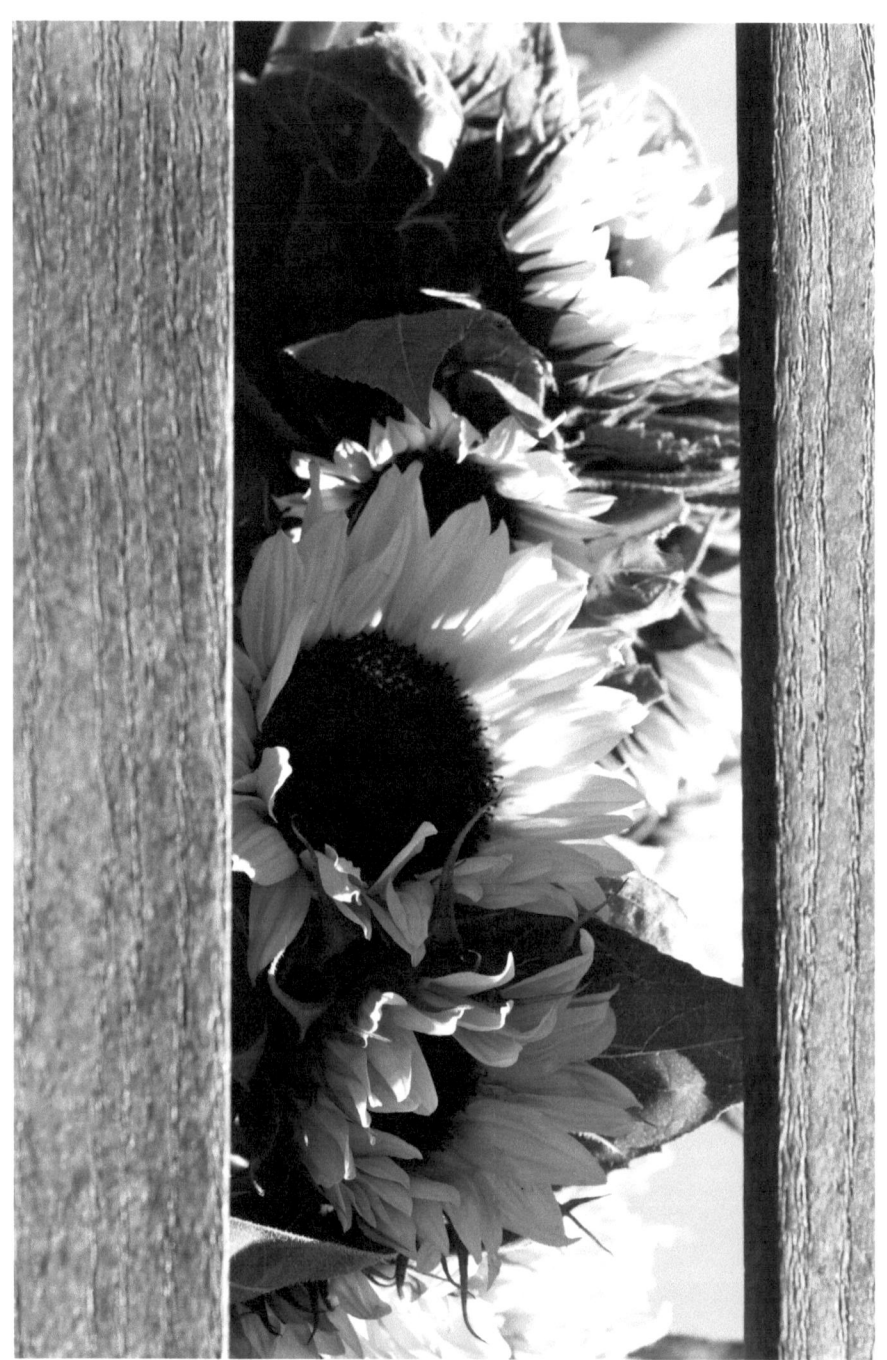

8345

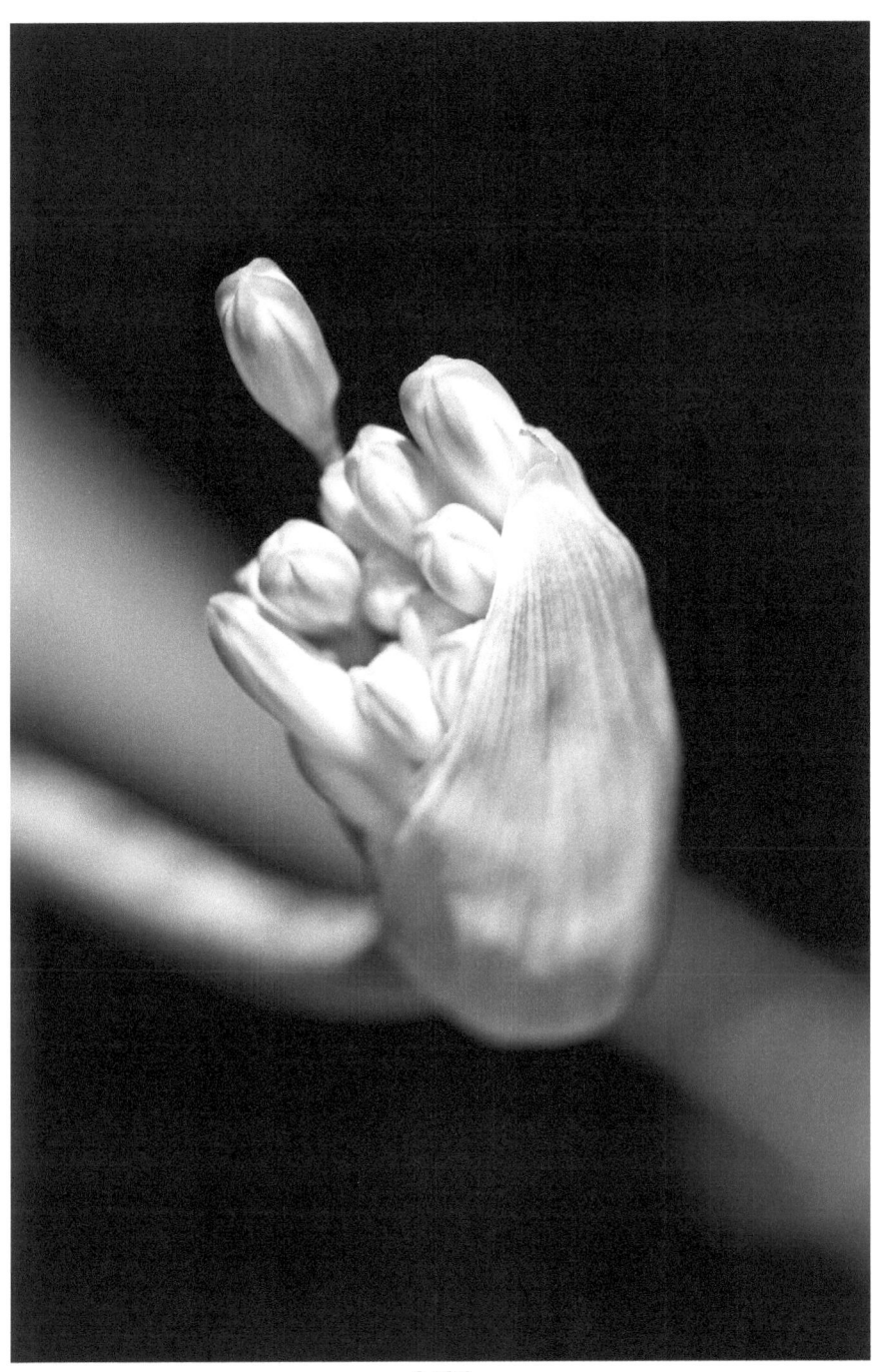

8407

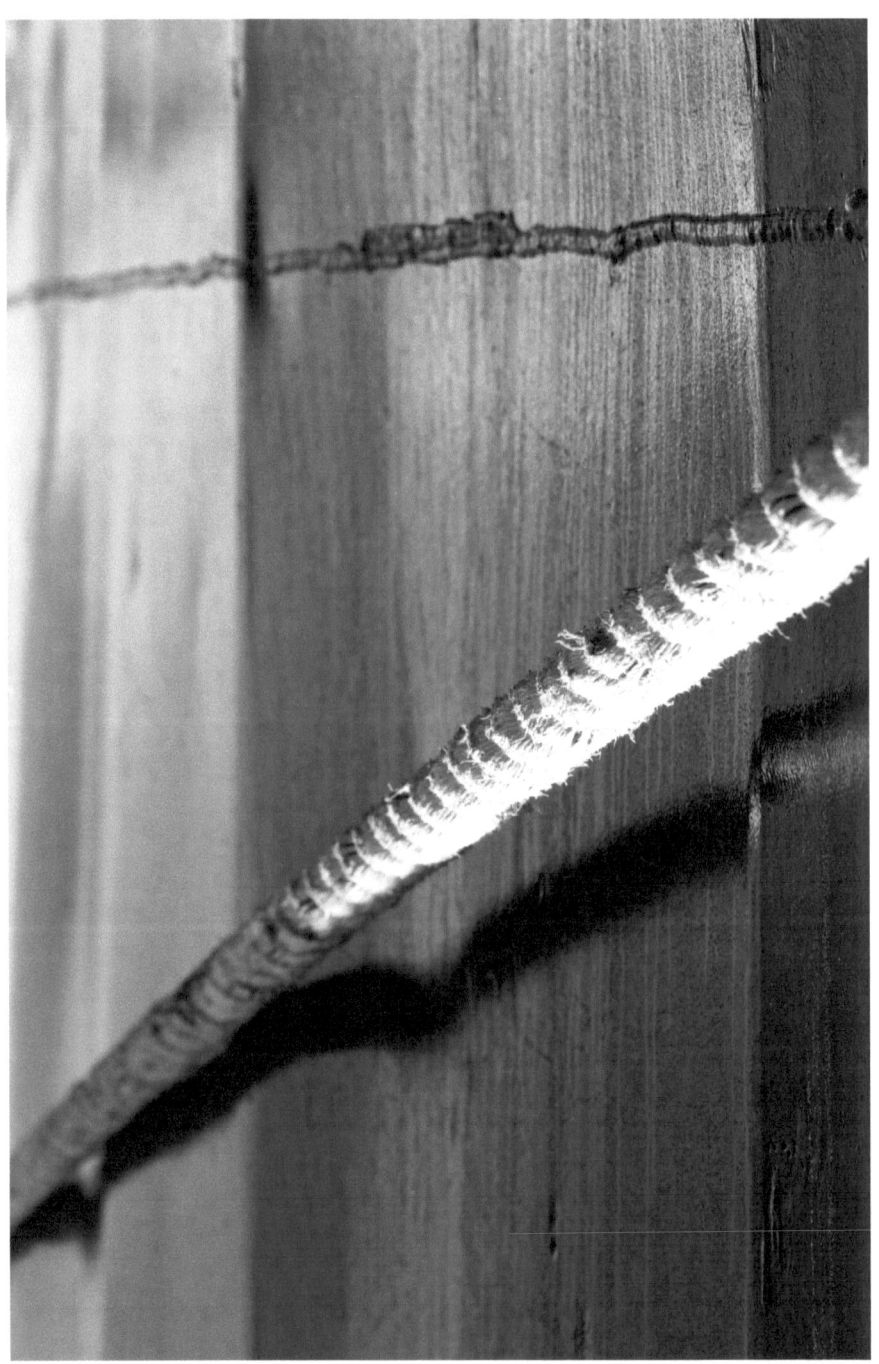

8470

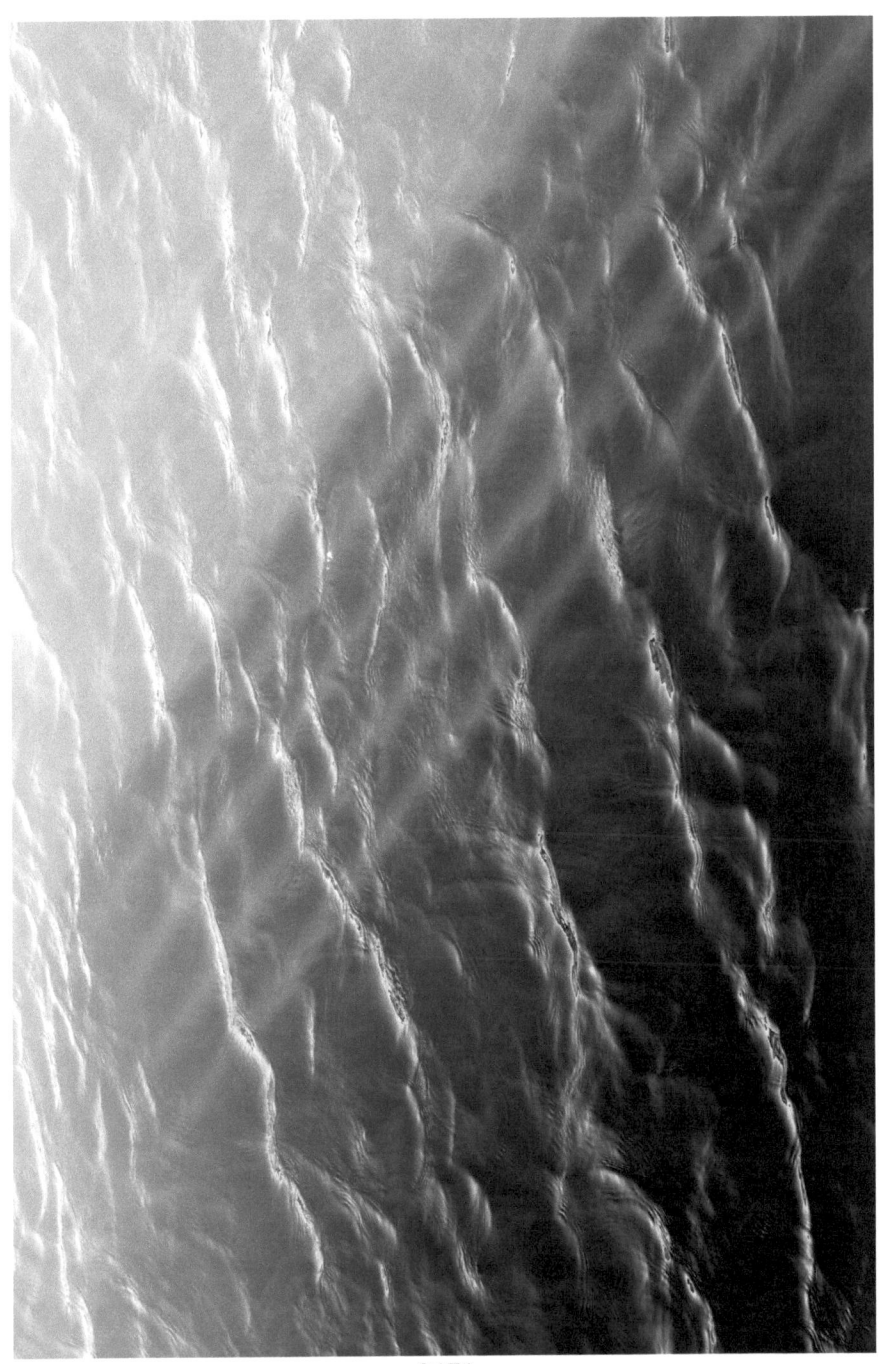

8471

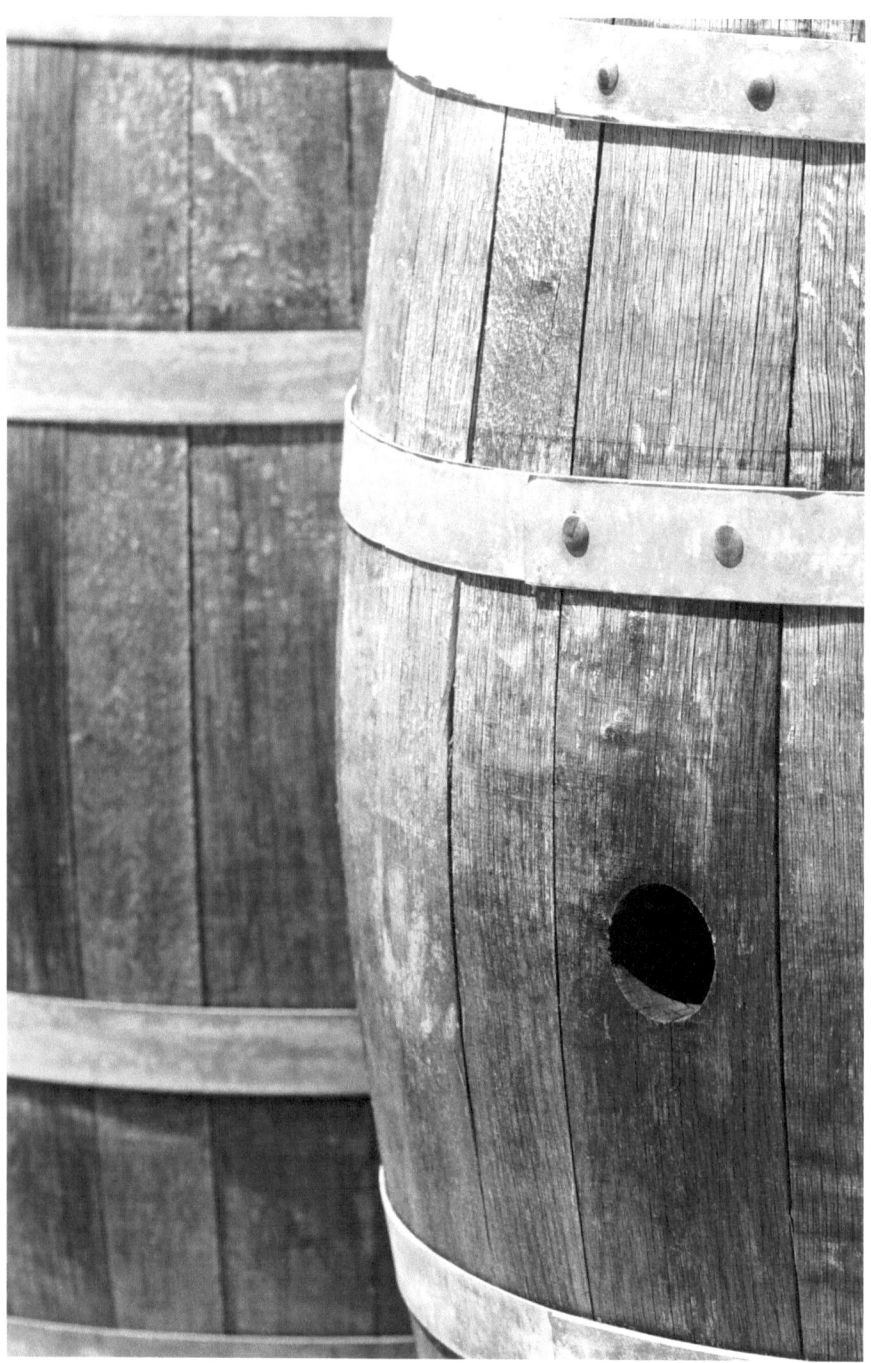

8815

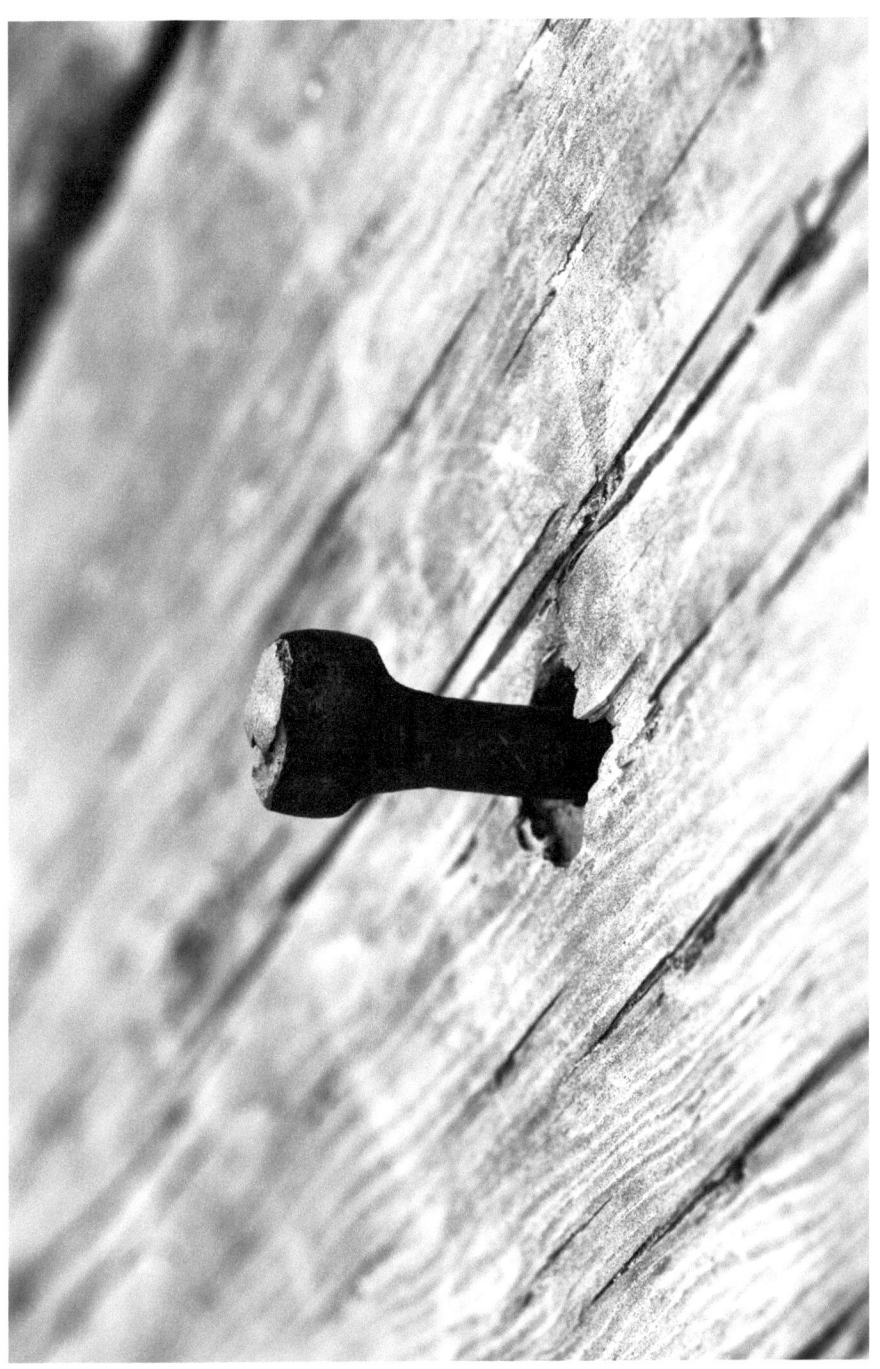

9024

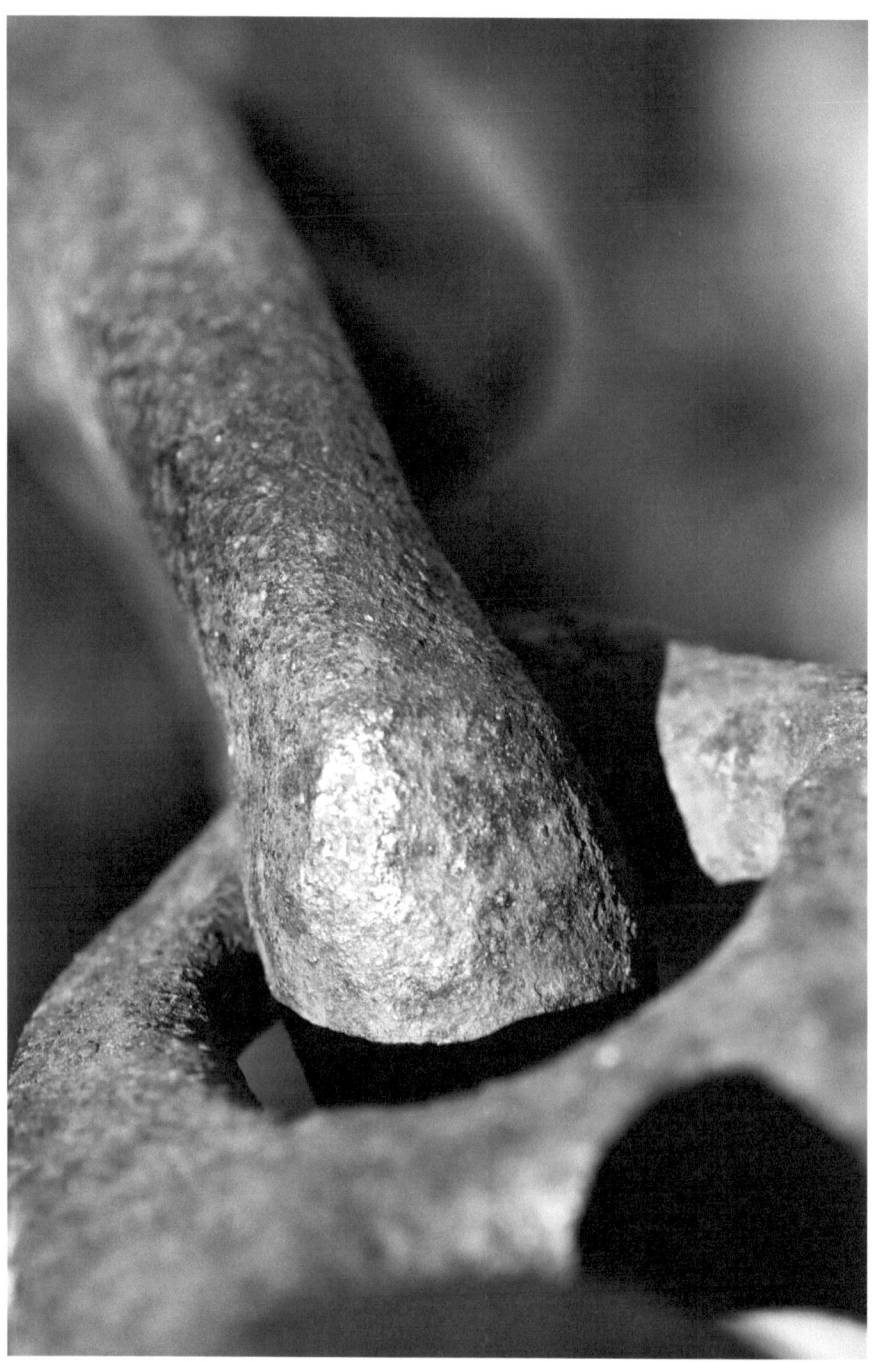

9353

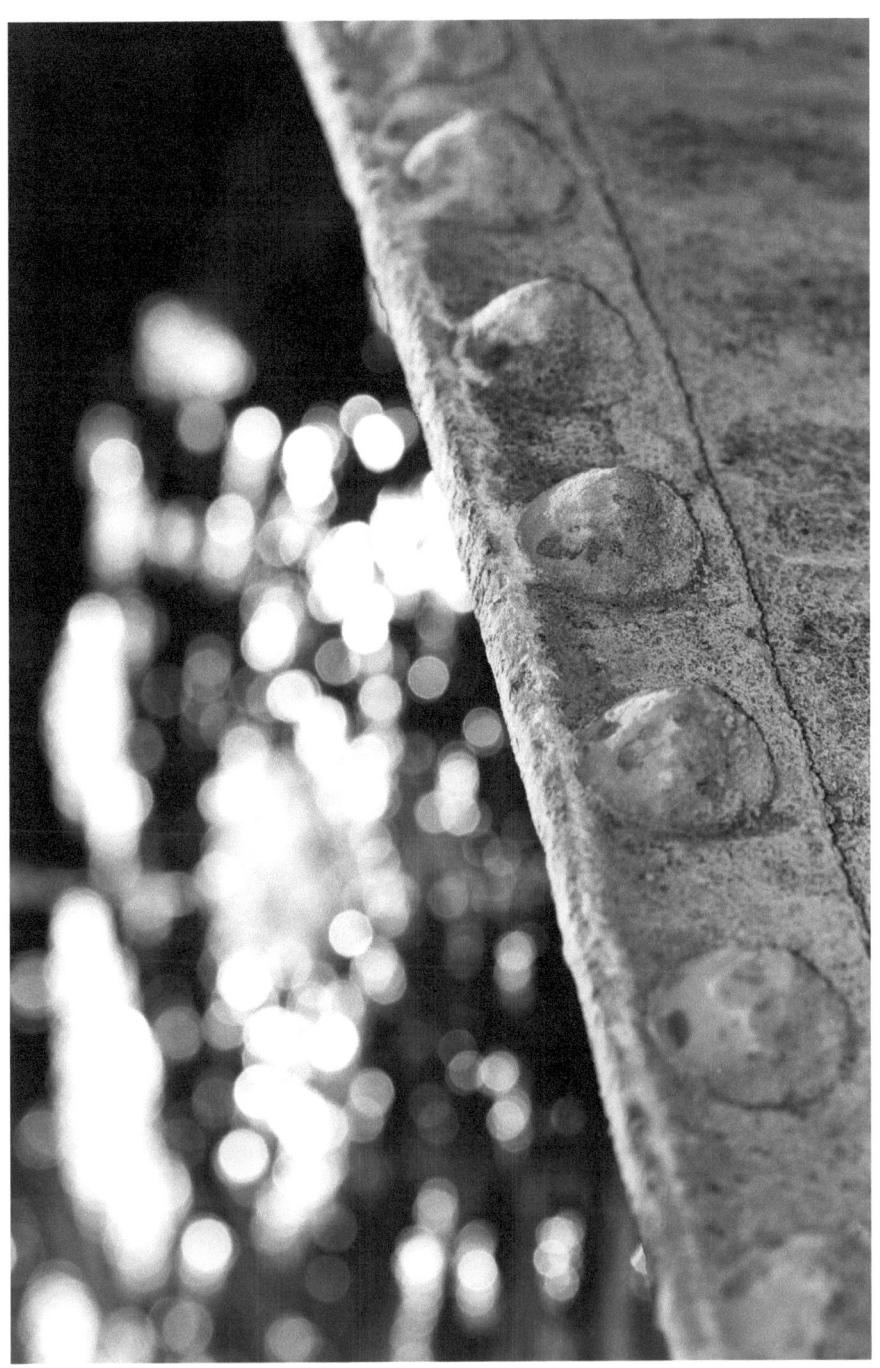

9430

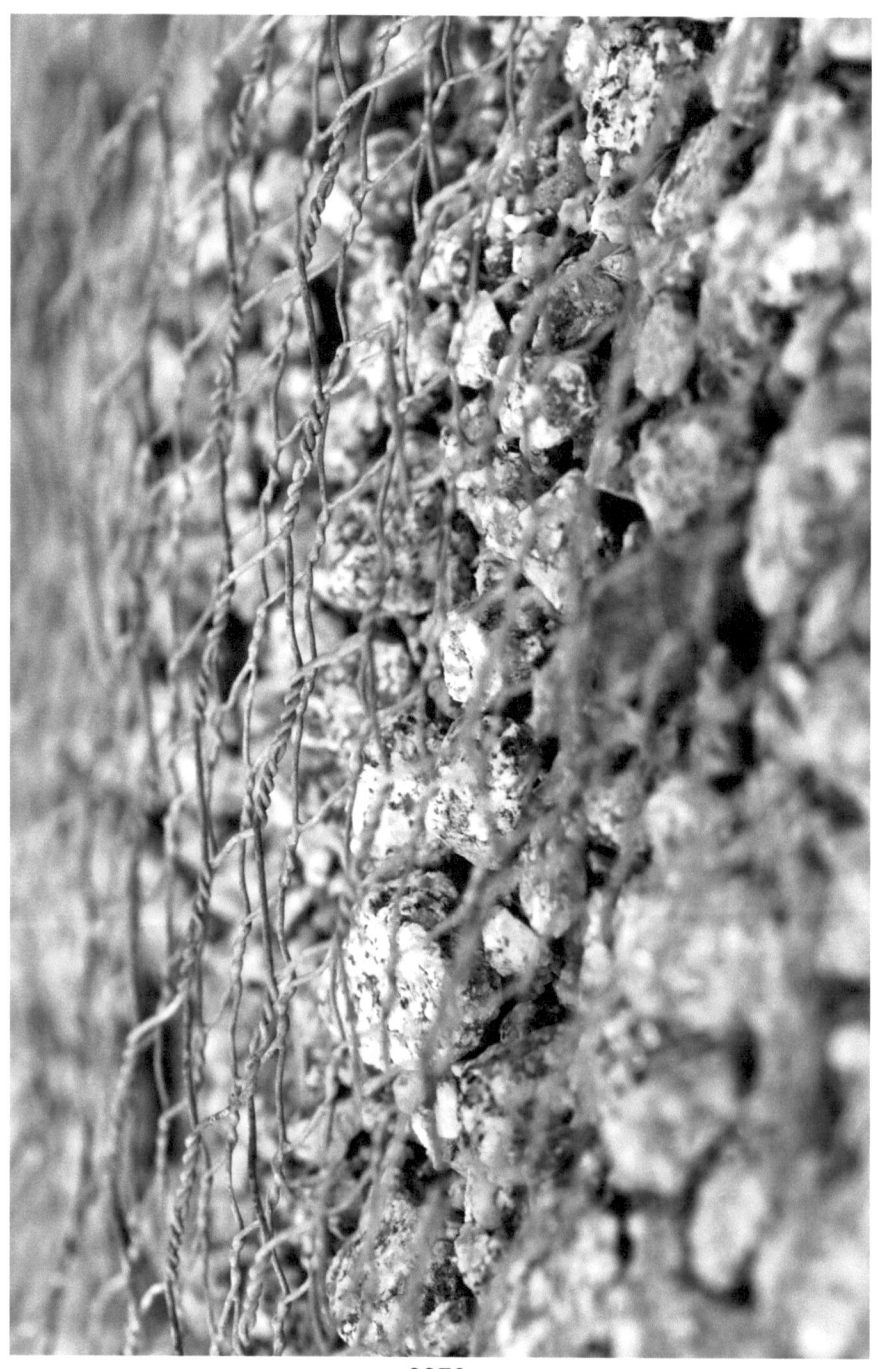

9970

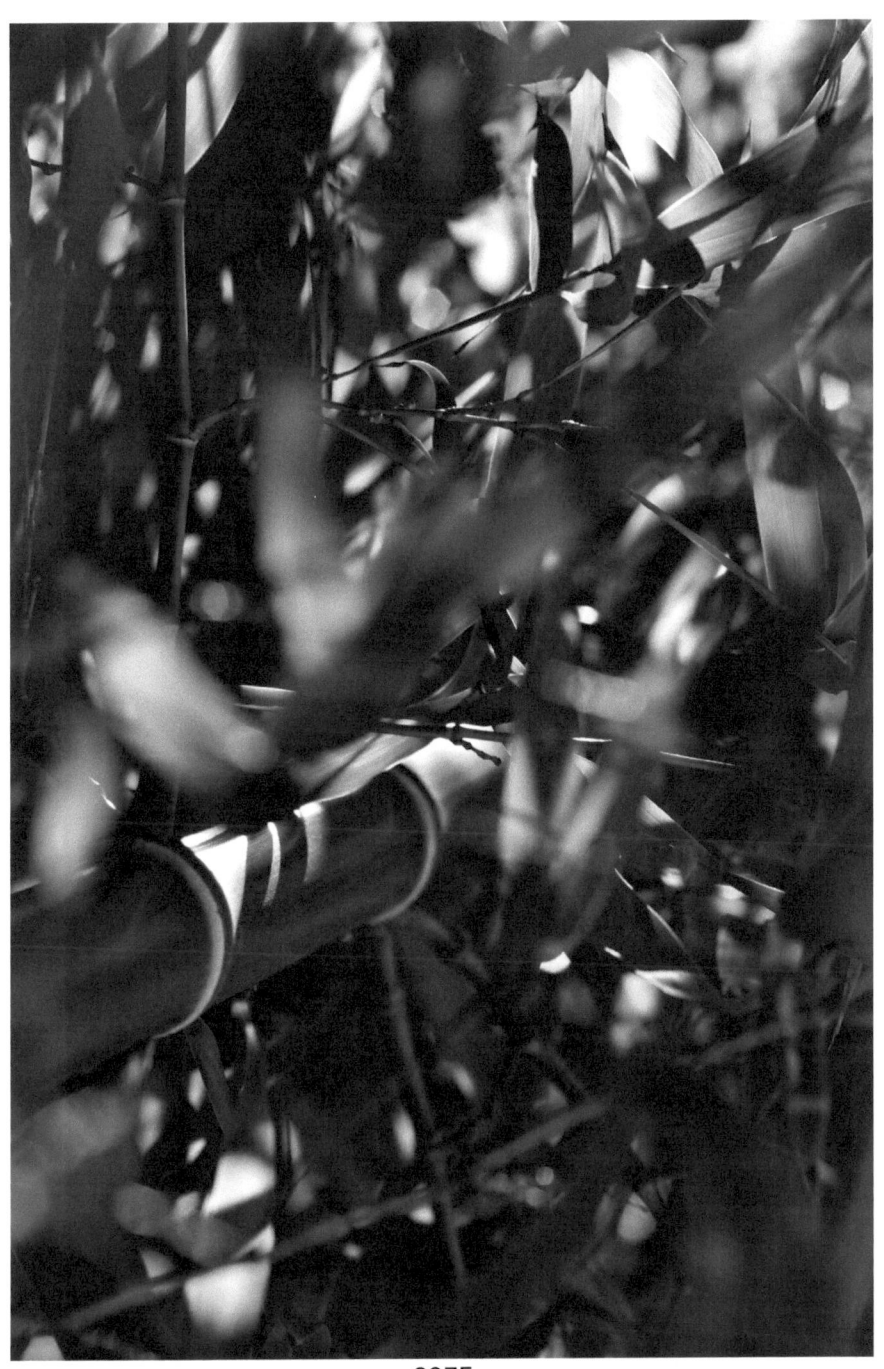

9975

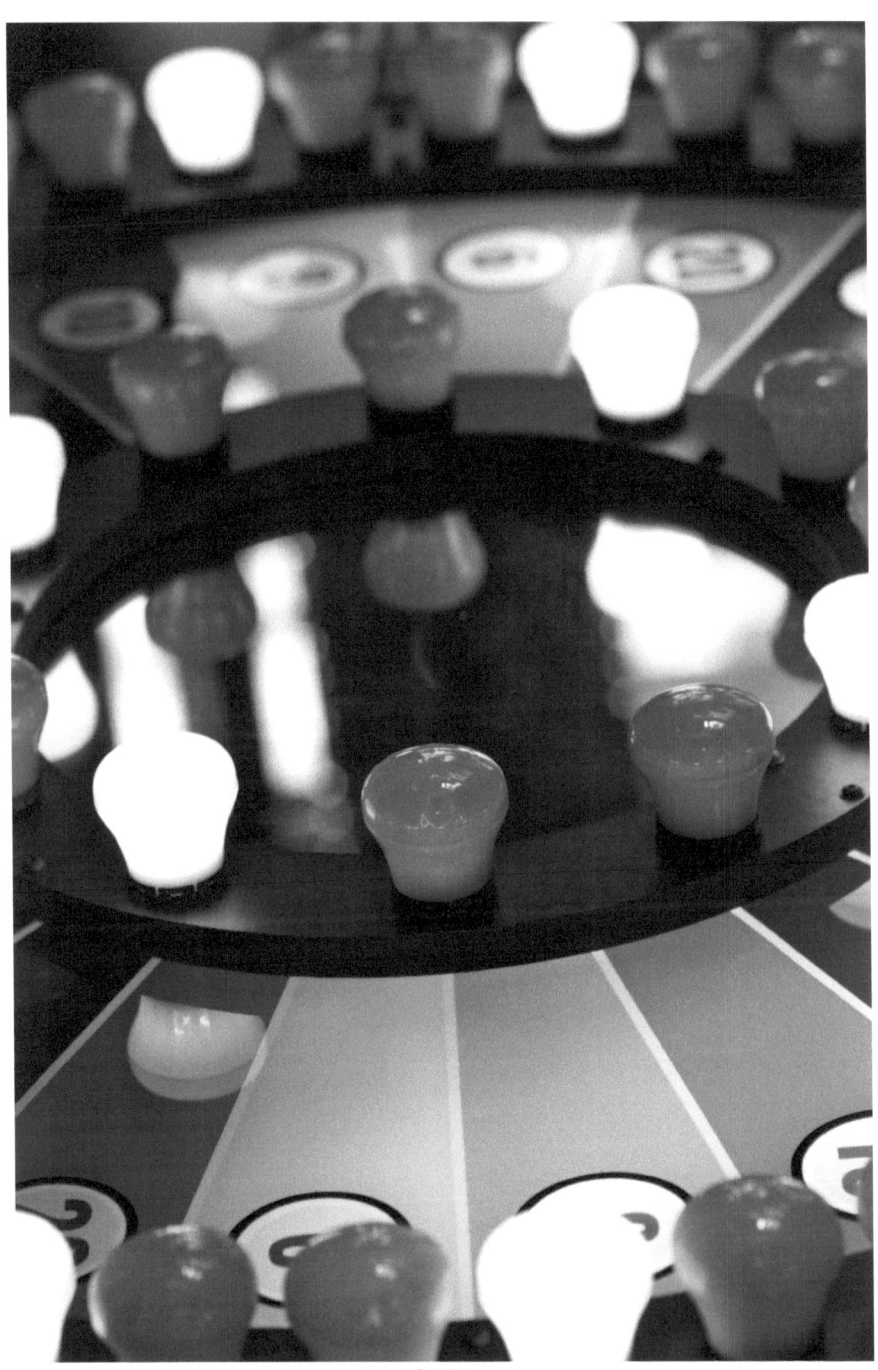

8471

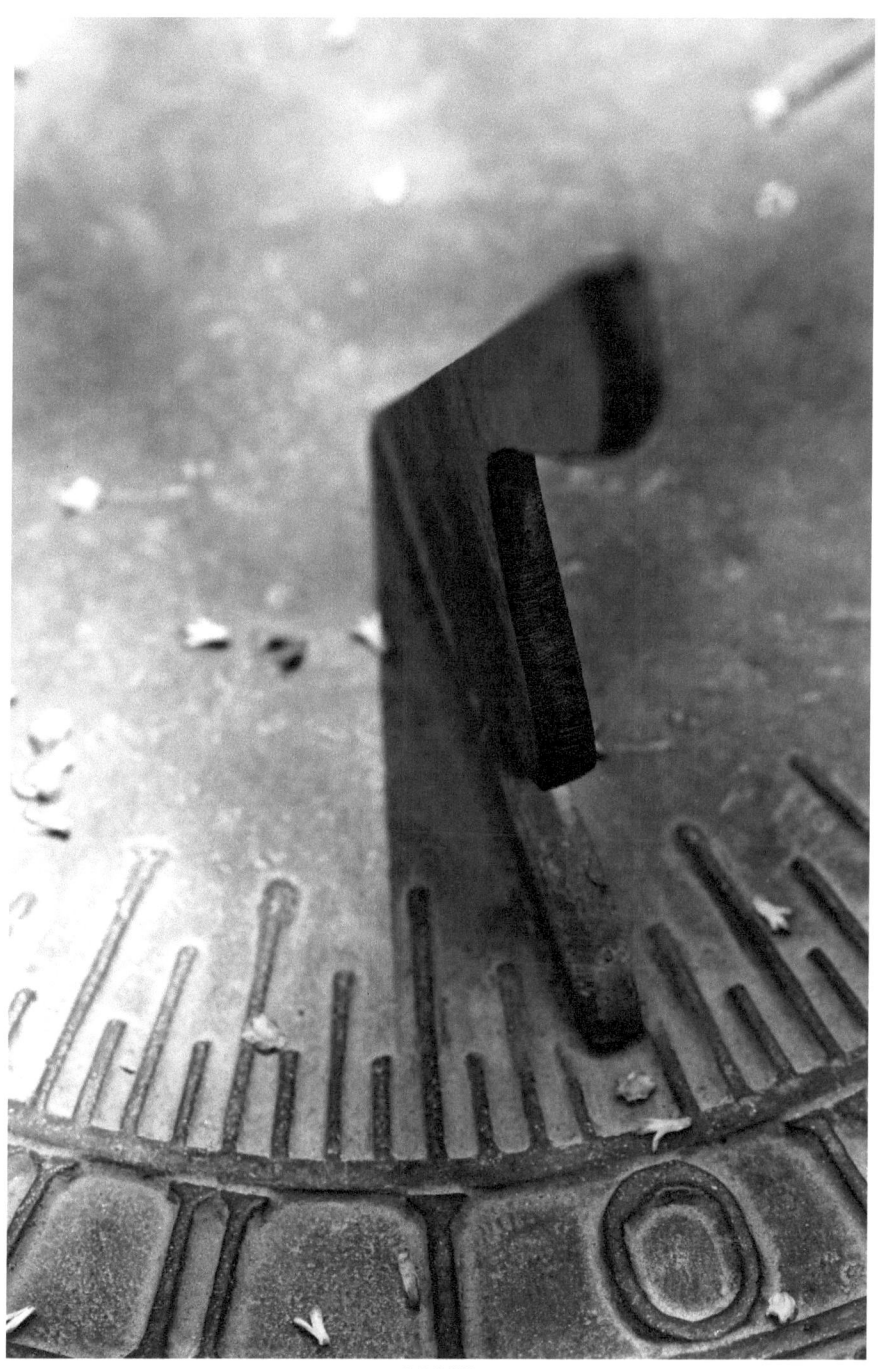

10002